THE ART OF SEEKING GOD

THE ART OF SEEKING GOD

AARON M. M. BUTLER

XULON ELITE PRESS

Xulon Press Elite
2301 Lucien Way #415
Maitland, FL 32751
407.339.4217
www.xulonpress.com

Unless otherwise indicated, Scripture quotations taken from the King
James Version (KJV) – *public domain.*

Printed in the United States of America.

Paperback ISBN-13: 978-1-63129-253-8
Ebook ISBN-13: 978-1-63129-254-5

This is for the home team! I love you all.

- ❖ Sherrell, Jeremiah, and Judah
- ❖ Prophet Cornelius Hale and First Lady Courtney Hale
- ❖ My parents and siblings
- ❖ The COD Family

All the glory belongs to God!
All the glory belongs to God!
(Mali Music signing voice)

Email: aaronmmbutler@gmail.com

Website: www.aaronmmbutler.com

Facebook: The Art of Seeking God

TABLE OF CONTENTS

Introduction ix

Chapter 1: Generation Of Seekers 1

Chapter 2: The Art Of Seeking God 9

Chapter 3: The Purpose Behind Seeking God. 17

Chapter 4: Seeking God Early 23

Chapter 5: Benefits To Seeking God Early 31

Chapter 6: In Spite Of, Don't Stop Seeking 43

Chapter 7: Drawbacks Of Not Seeking God 49

Chapter 8: The Greatest Seeker 55

Conclusion 65

Appendix A: Twelve Different Ways To Seek The Father 67

Appendix B: Benefits Of Fasting For The Natural Body 89

Notes 90

About The Author 91

Who, not what, you are seeking is seeking you.

Revised Quote, Aaron M. M. Butler

INTRODUCTION

At this pivotal time in history with so many questionable things taking place in the world, men and women of God that take kingdom action are in high demand. We live in an ever-changing world. Many people wonder about basic needs, terrorism, school shootings, police brutality, racism, poverty, and diversity. The values and morals that people live by change from culture to culture. There are different governments, organizations, and leaders that want different outcomes for the world in which we live.

Every day we witness some type of crime. We hear of heart-breaking stories, or we experience pain directly or indirectly. From community to community, there are some terrible things (addiction, murder, divorce, violence, discrimination, etc.) taking place.[1]

Ultimately, at the top level you have governments that are meeting with their counsel and putting solutions in place that you and I may or may not agree with. In all of this, the God of Abraham, Isaac, and Jacob has the hearts of the youngest, the oldest, the richest, the poorest, the wicked, and the purest in His hands. He is observing their intentions, words, and actions day and night. Times are dark and uncertain, but God has a solution that is bigger and better, and that plan involves the Christian church.

God is developing leaders like you and me to be a light in the midst of the earth where darkness, uncertainty, confusion, and ignorance are increasing.

Isaiah 60: 1-3 reads,

> "Arise, shine; for thy light is come; and the glory of the Lord is risen upon thee. For, behold, the darkness shall cover the earth, and gross darkness the people: but the Lord shall arise upon thee, and his glory shall be seen upon thee. And the Gentiles shall come to thy light, and kings to the brightness of thy rising."

God is raising up a body of believers who have the light of God in them and on them. The light of God, which is also the glory of God, will literally be on you and me in these last days. Those in darkness will see this light and they will be drawn to men and women of God. As this light begins to manifest on believers, unity will hit the body of Christ (1 Corinthians 12:27). We will be unified, walking in kingdom anointing, kingdom authority, and kingdom power. We will put kingdom strategies in place to address the problems humanity is facing. The one defining thing that we will have in common is that we will be God seekers that evolve into God pleasers.

Hebrews 11:5, 6 reads,

> "By faith Enoch was translated that he should not see death; and was not found, because God had translated him: for before his translation He had this testimony, that <u>He pleased God</u>. But without faith it is impossible to please Him, for He that cometh to God must believe that He is, and that He is a rewarder of them that diligently seek Him."

There are believers who are saved and committed to being in the presence or face of God. These believers will seek the thoughts of God, words of God, ways of God, and the will of God. The Bible makes it plain that when the people of God seek after God and are obedient to Him, then the blessings of God follow. The Bible makes it clear that seeking God can and will unlock the mysteries to the kingdom of God.

Mark 13:11 reads,

> "He answered and said unto them, because it is given unto you to know the mysteries of the kingdom of heaven, but to them it is not given."

INTRODUCTION

Jeremiah 33:3 reads,

> "Call unto me, and I will answer thee, and show thee
> great and mighty things, which thou knowest not."

Not only that, but there are also several spiritual benefits as
well as natural benefits that are bestowed upon those who seek
the kingdom of God.

Matthew 6:33 reads,

> "But seek ye first the kingdom of God, and his
> righteousness; and all these things shall be added
> unto you."

Seeking God can open up innumerable doors that lead to
spiritual and natural resources, skills, promotions, insights, growth,
development, and the list goes on and on.

The intentions of this book are to clearly state the true purpose
behind seeking God. In this book, we look at the art of seeking
God. "The art of" means the beauty of seeking God, the knowledge
or craft of seeking God, the field of seeking God, and the detailed
skills and techniques used to seek God. This book addresses the
spiritual and natural gains of seeking God as well as the drawbacks
of not seeking God. Several other truths about seeking God will
be addressed in this book, too.

Who is this book for? This book is for the new convert and the
seasoned saint. This book is for the rooted and grounded disciple
who just wants confirmation that he's on the right track. This book
is for the struggling and inconsistent believer who needs a push
to the next level of seeking God. This book is for the Christian
leader who wants to train his/her troops to seek God with *reckless
abandon*. This book is for the saint who is currently on the moun-
taintop receiving and hearing from God; and it is also for the saint
who is in the valley just trying to make the right decisions about
her next step in life.

My sincere prayer is that the words of this book will fall on
good ground (your heart) and bring a one-hundred-fold increase

into your life and the lives of those around you. I pray that, like the three Hebrew boys (Daniel 1:20), this book will make you ten times better in your understanding, knowledge, and wisdom as it pertains to seeking God. I pray that God will open the eyes of your understanding. I pray that God will awaken your inner ear to hear what the Spirit of God is saying to the church.

In the times that we live in, we need men and women of God who will seek God, hear from God, and bring a solution back to society that will empower the kingdom of God and the world in which we live. May God get all of the glory as you read and digest this book in Jesus' name! Amen!

VALUABLE POINTS TO LIVE BY:

- ❖ Men and women of God who take kingdom action are in high demand.
- ❖ The one defining thing that we will have in common is that we will be God seekers who evolve into God pleasers.
- ❖ This book will address the spiritual and natural gains of seeking God as well as the drawbacks of not seeking God.
- ❖ God is a rewarder of them who diligently seek Him.

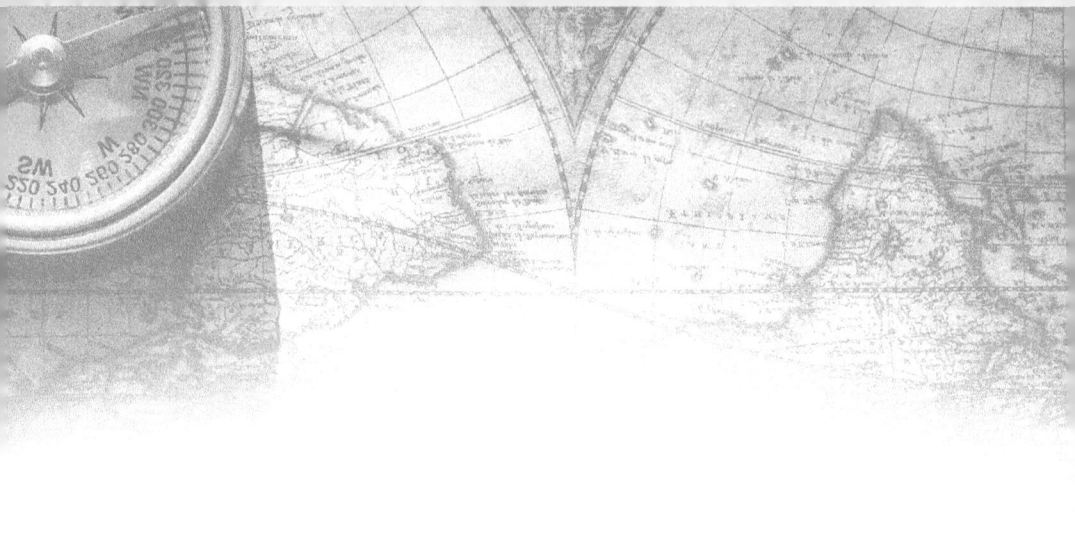

"I *put my heart and my soul into my work, and have lost my mind in the process.*"

Vincent van Gogh

CHAPTER 1

GENERATION OF SEEKERS

Matthew 6:33 reads,

> "But seek ye first the kingdom of heaven and His righteousness and all these things shall be added unto you."

God has raised up, and is raising up, warriors who are devoted to seeking the face of God, morning, noon, and night with reckless abandon. These seekers understand that all God has for them is wrapped up in the way they seek after God. The priority, and chief aim, is to first focus your whole being on seeking God and all that He has for you. When one seeks the kingdom of heaven and His righteousness, God is going to show one how to operate on earth from His point of view. As these warriors begin to seek God, the spiritual and natural blessings of God will be added to their lives.

If these seeking warriors had it their way, they would quit their jobs, school, and other responsibilities that hinder them from seeking the Father twenty-four hours a day and seven days a week. However, wisdom tells us that God needs relevant believers in key positions in our communities. Wisdom tells us that God is strategically placing His warriors around the globe in different places of influence that range from the medical field to the music industry, from the educational field to the technology field, from the sports world to the political world. He needs believers who are ready to rule like Joseph and not be easily influenced like Judas Iscariot.

While true believers will never forsake the assembly of saints coming together, there is a deeper understanding that we are called to occupy the earth until the return of Jesus Christ. The days of Christians *only* wanting to go to church, *only* wanting to establish

1

churches, *only* wanting to have revivals and conferences, giving the earth and the fullness thereof to the world are over. God has seeking warriors who are taking position across the land with the intention of possessing and occupying the land.

The Christians of today, like the Christians in the first-century church, are relevant to humanity. We are called to be all things to all people. We are called to solve problems in the natural and spiritual realms. We are called to set up the kingdom of heaven in the earth. That means that when one of us enters a city, the people of that city will know that there are Christians who are invested in every facet of that community. Any given city will have businesses and organizations that are Christian-owned and operated by the best minds that society has to offer. We will have a standard, but we will not discriminate. All will know where we stand when it comes to God, but they will feel the love of God. Christians will be in prominent positions, but we will have a heart for people, a love for humanity, and a fire to establish the kingdom of heaven.

One virtue that these seeking warriors possess is the zeal of the Lord. The zeal of the Lord will trigger this end-time move of God that has taken place, is taking place, and will take place in the earth. What exactly is the zeal of the Lord? Let's look at a couple of scriptures.

Isaiah 9:7 reads,

> "Of the increase of his government and peace there shall be no end, upon the throne of David, and upon His of kingdom, to order it, and to establish it with judgment and with justice from henceforth even forever. The zeal of the Lord of hosts will perform this."

Isaiah 37:32 reads,

> "For out of Jerusalem shall go forth a remnant, and they that escape out of mount Zion: the zeal of the Lord of hosts shall do this."

Jesus will have a governmental kingdom in the earth that branches off into all facets of society. The zeal of the Lord will fuel this end-time movement. The definition of zeal in the Hebrew is: jealousy; envy; to be jealous or envious of, to make jealous; to move to jealousy; to provoke to jealousy; to excite to jealous anger, to provoke to jealous anger.[1] The zeal of the Lord speaks of a jealousy for the things of God, a longing, a heat or burning for the things of God to be in place, indignation for the things of God, or an extreme loyalty to see the things of God manifested and established in the earth.

The zeal of the Lord is a deep-rooted, jealous anger that provokes one to work. The zeal of the Lord provokes one to action. The zeal of the Lord will provoke you to do something that will strategically transform a person, a family, a city, or a nation.

- ❖ Zealous Christians operate with the same wisdom that Jesus operated with when He did His earthly ministry a little over 2,000 years ago.
- ❖ Zealous Christians want to see mankind saved from their sins and saved to their purpose.
- ❖ Zealous Christians want to see the God kingdom established and not the current system that is religious and not kingdom focused.
- ❖ Zealous Christians want to see godly leaders in place, not leaders who put laws in place that go against the Holy Bible.
- ❖ Zealous Christians want to see God's government in place and not the governments of this world where people suffer at the hands of corrupt leaders and corrupt systems.

The book of Nehemiah is a prime example of zealous people at work. Let's strive to be zealous Christians.

Isaiah 59:17 reads,

> "For he put on righteousness as a breastplate, and
> an helmet of salvation upon his head; and he put
> on the garments of vengeance for clothing, and was
> clad with zeal as a cloak."

A cloak is a cape, a robe, a covering, an outer garment, a mantle, etc. In this verse, zeal is a protective covering that was placed over the other clothing that was upon the Lord. Therefore, the Lord had on a cape of zeal. This zeal speaks of a furious divine jealously (AMPC). Zeal is a divine burning, a passionate desire to see the will of God accomplished in the right timing of God. Anything that gets in the way of the will of God being established will stir up the zeal of the Lord for the things of God.

Why a cape of zeal? The zeal is a cloak or cape of passionate burning for the things of God. The zeal of the Lord is constantly pushing us to do the work of the Lord regardless of what your family may say, what other believers around you may say, what the enemies around you may say, what the weather is trying to do, what your mind is telling you, who betrays you, and what the devil is trying to do. Are you ready for the zeal of the Lord to flare up inside of you? Receive it now!

It was zeal that pushed Moses to confront the evil Pharaoh who thought he could control the children of Israel. The zeal of Lord empowered Samson to defeat the Philistines time and time again. The zeal of the Lord ignited the fire inside of Joshua to defeat the enemies possessing the Promised Land. The zeal of the Lord also surfaced in men and women of God, like Daniel, Nehemiah, Esther, and many others. The zeal of the Lord provoked men and women of God to do mighty exploits in the Bible days and will once again provoke men and women of God to do mighty exploits in the day and age in which we live.

Isaiah 63:15 reads,

> "Look down from heaven, and behold from the habitation of thy holiness and of thy glory: where is thy zeal and thy strength, the sounding of thy bowels and of thy mercies toward me? Are they restrained?"

In this verse, zeal speaks of God's jealousy (AMPC). The children of Judah were asking God, "Where is your zeal for the things of God?" They were crying out to God telling Him that He did not perform the way He did in the past. They were saying, "Why are you holding back your zeal?"

God is releasing His zeal to end time warriors. The zeal of the Lord is a deep, burning jealousy that is totally focused on establishing the kingdom of God in the earth. The zeal of the Lord is divine, and the carnal mind cannot understand it.

These end-time warriors who seek the face of God have the zeal to tear down the devil's kingdom and plenty of zeal to establish the kingdom of God. These seeking warriors have a zeal to raise the dead literally, as well as spiritually. They have enough zeal to cast out devils and to heal the sick. They have enough zeal to conduct themselves in a holy, righteous, and godly manner in private and in public. These zealous warriors are spiritual enough to prophesy and hear from God, but they are also in tune with mankind enough to conduct a business meeting that offers solutions to mankind's problems. These warriors have an overflow of zeal to walk in the fear of God, love of God, compassion of God, humility of God, anointing of God, and authority of God. These warriors have an ear to hear and a will to be obedient to the voice of God, even unto death. These zealous warriors have "a new heart" and are in the process of renewing their minds daily.

One thing these warriors do that separates them from the other Bible-believing Christians is *seek the face of God*. Seeking God has many levels to it. The seeking can be done individually or corporately, but the bottom line is that these warriors are disciplining themselves to seek God consistently and diligently with all reverence. They are scheduling their lives around seeking God. These seeking warriors know and understand that consistent seeking leads to a deeper relationship of intimacy with the Father. Psalm 24:6 reads,

> "This is the generation of them that seek him, that seek thy face, O Jacob. Selah."

The Bible speaks of a generation that seeks the face of God. That generation is a generation of warriors that is seeking to become the Christ, in full capacity. Christians are ready and willing to be glorified that the Father might be glorified in them and through them. They are going to be the Christ, the body of believers that walks in the fullness of God. (See Revelation 11:15 and Revelation 12:10) This generation of seekers has an ear to hear God, but is also relevant to humanity. They are focused on pleasing God and making society better on all levels.

Zechariah 8:20-23 reads,

> Thus saith the LORD of hosts; It shall yet come to pass, that there shall come people, and the inhabitants of many cities: And the inhabitants of one city shall go to another, saying, Let us go speedily to pray before the LORD, and to seek the LORD of hosts: I will go also. Yea, many people and strong nations shall come to seek the LORD of hosts in Jerusalem, and to pray before the LORD. Thus saith the LORD of hosts; In those days it shall come to pass, that ten men shall take hold out of all languages of the nations, even shall take hold of the skirt of him that is a Jew, saying, We will go with you: for we have heard that God is with you.

The above verses speak of a people from all ethnic groups that will hasten to seek God, not for personal or group benefits, but because they want an audience with God. These seekers want to commune with God. They want to be in His presence and He in theirs. These seekers understand that only God can meet their needs. The above verses speak of the rich and the poor, the young and the old, the strong and the weak, the wise and the foolish recognizing that they have a void in their life that only God can fill. These verses speak of seekers seeking those who have been seeking God and connecting with God. These verses speak of a glory that is upon seekers that religious people have desired for ages. Seekers have an attracting or drawing anointing that draws people to them.

God has people who want to follow you because they can see that God is with you. God's hand is upon you and humans can sense the call of God on your life. They will either draw closer to you or retreat. Look for divine encounters. Be ready for them. God has raised up, and is raising up, warriors who seek the face of God for such a time as this. Right now, humanity is seeking something that will satisfy them spiritually. Seekers, let us remain true to Jesus so that when those who are seeking cross our path, we will be a Tree of Life to them and not a Tree of Knowledge.

Now prepare yourself, for in the next several chapters I am going to lay out to you what God has placed in my spirit concerning the art of seeking God. Understand that this book is just a small fraction of what it really means to seek God. Shallow Christians, dive into the depth of this book. Deep Christians, take this book to a deeper level. But I beseech all who read this book, "Seek the face of God!" Amen!

VALUABLE POINTS TO LIVE BY:

- ❖ Consistent seeking leads to a deeper relationship of intimacy with the Father.
- ❖ God seekers have an attracting or drawing anointing that draws people to them.

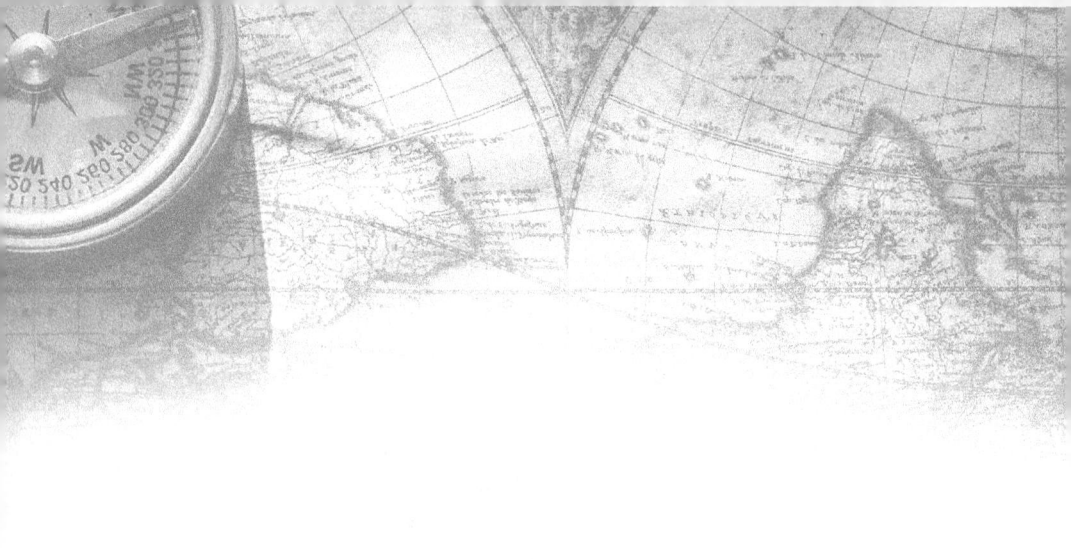

"*The mystery of seeking God is that HE is the One who finds you.*"

Kingsley Opuwari Manuel

CHAPTER 2

THE ART OF SEEKING GOD

1 Chronicles 16:11 reads,

> "Seek the Lord and his strength, seek his face continually."

Matthew 7:7, 8 reads,

> "Ask, and it shall be given you; seek, and ye shall find, knock, and it shall be open unto you: For every one that asketh receiveth; and he that seeketh findeth; and to him that knocketh it shall be opened."

Isaiah 55:6 reads,

> "Seek ye the Lord while he may be found, call ye upon him while he is near."

Based on the above scriptures, the Bible plainly states that seeking God is mandatory for every believer. There are countless examples of God-fearing men and women who sought after God in the Bible all throughout the day and night. These men and women sought after God by different methods. Their lives were centered on pleasing God, being obedient to the will of God, and fulfilling their purpose in God. The saints in the Scripture were successful because they had one thing in common: the backbone of their sainthood was rooted and grounded in seeking God. Daniel was a man of God who sought the Lord in prayer on a consistent basis. David was a praise and worship warrior who established a culture of seeking the Lord twenty-four hours a day for seven days a week. Enoch sought after God in such a way that eventually God took him to be His own (Genesis 5:18-24). These saints understood what it meant to seek God.

Let's review the question, "What is the art of seeking God?" When I hear the word *art*, I think of someone with a skillset to do something or create something that inspires others to want to do the same thing or something similar. The word art deals with what is beautiful, expressive, perfect, next level, the best of, or the quality of. *Art* is also defined as a genre, a field of study, any field using skills and techniques of art, a branch of learning, skill in conducting any human activity, the principles or methods of governing any branch of learning.[1] For the purpose of this book, art deals with using principles, methods, and expression in a set field of study that focuses on God.

The word *seeking* means to go in search of, to try to find by searching or questioning, try to locate or discover; search for, hunt, to go to, to ask, to make an effort to find something or someone; set one's sight upon. For the purpose of this book, seeking deals with making an effort to know, to find or discover God by any means necessary.

The Art of Seeking God is focused on using principles, methods, and expression, to know and discover God on a greater level that leads to more intimacy with Him and His body. All that the body of Christ has done up to this point has been good, but God is demanding more. This book deals with strategically seeking after God and finding all that God has for us that will make us mature and productive Christians. As we seek His face, He will give us direction on how more of Him can be released into the earth.

Before giving a deeper explanation as to what it means to seek God, I want to look at some seeking examples. Let me paint this picture so that you can understand where we are about to voyage to in this book.

I am positive that many of you at some point have lost your car keys or house keys. When the keys are lost, you seek or search for them. You will look under the bed, behind the couch, in every room, crack, and cranny. Sometimes as you look, you get impatient and irritable, but you keep looking. Then, if you still do not find them, you might ask someone, "Have you seen my keys?" If they say they haven't, then you keep looking. You try to retrace your steps. As you seek, you are focused only on finding the keys. Sometimes you will stop, sit down, and ponder about where you had them last. Then you continue seeking until you find them. Once you find them, you regain your peace and calmness returns to you, because now you can do what you intended to do before losing or misplacing your keys.

Another example of seeking is when you search for a topic on the internet. You type in your topic and a list of sites related to your topic comes up on the screen. Then you browse and start clicking on different websites. Sometimes your topic will come up and sometimes you get something with the right words but a different topic. At other times, you find your topic but then you realize that you need more information on the topic. The search continues until you find the right amount of information to satisfy your needs. Once you find what you are looking for, you feel content and ready to move on to the next thing on your agenda.

When it comes to the art of seeking God, that is not the case. You can never move on to the next item on your agenda because God *is* the agenda. He is the centerpiece on the table that everyone is talking about. He is the foundational cornerstone for all humanity. *The Art of Seeking God* is a book that provides people with practical ways to seek God.

When seeking God and His kingdom, we are talking about the GREAT SEEK that never ends. I am using the phrase GREAT SEEK because, no matter how much the Lord tells you, reveals to you, or shows you, there is always more of God to be revealed. The wisdom of God, the knowledge of God, the things of God, and the ways of God are infinite. God always has more to give to those who seek Him. I am also using the phrase GREAT SEEK because you will not find all of God overnight. The GREAT SEEK will require you to labor.

The word *labor* means to work. Work is not always easy. Sometimes, work can be fun and at other times work can be very hard. Once you have labored for a season, then you must continue to labor.

Seeking God must be done on a consistent basis. Your strength or daily bread is in your seeking. The Bible states in 2 Thessalonians

3:10, "…that if a man does not work then he should not eat." If you do not put the work into seeking God, then do not expect your table to be full of spiritual and natural blessings. One of the most powerful principles in the Bible says that whatsoever a man soweth, that shall he also reap. Read Galatians 6:7-9. Sowing is talking about planting seeds and reaping is talking about gathering. When we seek God, we are planting seeds and cultivating seeds that lead to deeper roots. When the harvest comes, those seeds will manifest into something fruitful and we will begin to walk in the fullness of God. When we seek God, we invest in ourselves. The more you put into seeking God, the more you will get out of God.

We plant seeds or scatter seeds into the soil of our hearts when we seek God. Once you sow the seeds, then you must cultivate the seeds. Cultivating is talking about forming and refining. Cultivation is done when you consistently water your seeds. In other words, you have to add godly knowledge onto godly knowledge, godly wisdom onto godly wisdom, godly understanding onto godly understanding, revelation onto revelation, prayer onto prayer, meditation onto meditation, reading onto reading, studying onto studying, love onto love, etc. You must continue to build upon what you know and experience.

As you cultivate your seeds in your heart daily and weekly, eventually you will develop a consistent, intimate relationship with the Holy Ghost. Relationship and intimacy with the Father is the number one goal of seeking God. You must continue to build upon what you know and experience. When you sow to the Spirit, God will not disappoint you. (Galatians 6:7-9). Then, once those seeds blossom and manifest into fruit, you must *still* seek God. God will always have something to tell you, show you, and reveal to you.

John 16:12-13 reads,

> "I have yet many things to say to unto you, but ye cannot bear them now. Howbeit when he, the Spirit of truth, is come, he will guide you into all truth: for he shall not speak of himself; but whatsoever he shall hear, that shall he speak: and he will show you things to come."

I had a dream years ago and God showed me something profound. He showed me a huge, white wall. The wall had thousands of squares on it. The thousands of squares were symbolic of God's knowledge. God spoke into my spirit that the knowledge of man only equals one of those squares. He showed me that the brightest, most intelligent person who walks in the deepest and highest revelatory word is still ignorant compared to what God knows.

I had another dream. In this dream, in a room, I saw information just lying around all over the floor. The information was contained in boxes and packages. God spoke in my spirit that He had things He wanted to share with His people, but they would only receive the information when they started seeking Him consistently. The GREAT SEEK must not end because God wants to reveal His will to us so we can stay relevant to the current generation and future generations.

Seeking God is a lifestyle that you can never retire from. Seeking God is a mandatory mandate for every believer. Will you feel like seeking God every day? The answer is, yes and no. Matthew 26:41 tells us, "…the spirit is willing but the flesh is weak." The spirit desires, hungers, and thirsts after the things of God. The flesh, on the other hand, is opposed to God. (Psalm 42:1, 2)

There are several ways to seek God. I will briefly give and explain some of the ways to seek God. Understand, God does not and never will lie. If His Word says it, then we must embrace it, move by faith, and act according to His Word. We are learning about the art of seeking God and part of that deals with the "how to." It is great to hear and learn, but if you never learn "how to," then how can you truly experience seeking God? It is great to hear about another's experience with seeking God, but I want you to experience all of God in public and private. The experiences with God start with you seeking God, or at least learning *how* to seek God. As you experience God, you will become a stronger Christian. You will grow spiritually and "become Christ" in the earth. As you seek God and experience Him, you will have similar stories to men and women in the Bible.

❖ Like Moses, you and I will deal with the Pharaohs

of the land.

❖ Like Joseph, we will solve major problems.
❖ Like Joshua, we will defeat the enemies of God.
❖ Like David, we will slay giants.
❖ Like Nehemiah, we will build the waste places.
❖ Like Esther, we will be pure before the King.
❖ Like Peter, we will heal people with our shadows.
❖ Like Samuel, we will prophesy.
❖ Like Paul, we will teach and preach.
❖ Like Jeremiah, we will stand flat-footed and speak what "Thus saith the Lord."
❖ Like Josiah, we will live by the Word of God.

We will be the offspring of Jesus and do greater works like He spoke of. All of this will result from us seeking God and spending time with the Holy Spirit. See Appendix A for ways to seek God and the application behind how to seek God. For example, it will detail how to seek God by reading the Word of God, studying the Word of God, praying, praising God, worshipping God, meditating, listening to music, and more.

You must have a balance when you seek God. That is part of the art of seeking God. You must know the ways to seek God and use those ways to seek God as the Spirit of God leads you. You can never pray enough. You can never read and study the Word of God enough. You can never meditate on, praise, and worship the Father enough. Seeking God consistently can help keep your motives pure, rooted and grounded in love. God wants seekers who mature into trees of life and not trees of knowledge, which are really trees of death.

The Holy Ghost is waiting to meet you when you begin to seek the Father. The Holy Ghost wants to help and guide you into all truth (revelation, insight, data, direction, etc.). The Bible says, seek the Lord while He may be found. Be diligent and consistent in seeking after God.

1 Chronicles 28:9 states,

"And thou, Solomon my son, know thou the God

of thy father, and serve him with a perfect heart and with a willing mind: for the LORD searcheth all hearts, and understandeth all the imaginations of the thoughts: if thou seek him, he will be found of thee; but if thou forsake him, he will cast thee off forever."

God is waiting for sincere seekers who will seek Him consistently without any secret agendas or hidden motives. For if we seek the Holy Ghost, we will find Him.

The Bible says that God resides with those of a broken, contrite, and humble spirit (Isaiah 57:15). The spirit of humility is one of the keys to successful seeking. Humility is when the flesh lets go and allows the Spirit of God to take total control to direct the spirit of man. When you seek the Holy Ghost, be obedient to what, when, where, and how He wants you to seek Him.

Discipline is one of the keys to success. Discipline means self-control. Discipline is training that is expected to produce a specific character or pattern of behavior that leads to moral, mental, and spiritual improvement. We were made in the image and likeness of God. Through sincere seeking, the image and likeness of God can become a daily-manifested reality in our lives. May you seek God diligently, consistently, and in peace with bulldog tenacity! Amen!

VALUABLE POINTS TO LIVE BY:

- ❖ *The Art of Seeking God* is focused on using principles, methods, and expressions to know and discover God on a greater level that leads to more intimacy with Him and His body.
- ❖ If you do not put the work into seeking God, then do not expect your table to be full of spiritual and natural blessings.
- ❖ When we seek God, we invest in ourselves. The more you put into seeking God, the more you will get out of God.
- ❖ The experiences with God start with you seeking God, or at least learning *how* to seek God (see Appendix A).

Art is meant to disturb, science reassures.

Georges Braque

CHAPTER 3

THE PURPOSE BEHIND SEEKING GOD

When Jesus came down to earth there was a purpose behind seeking the Father. The more He sought the Father, the more He realized that **there was a purpose for His life**. Each time that He sought the Father, He received more power to complete the task that He was purposed to do in the earth. His purpose was multifold, but not limited to:

- ❖ His baptism
- ❖ Identifying the twelve disciples
- ❖ Preaching and teaching the kingdom of God
- ❖ Operating in supernatural gifts
- ❖ Giving gifts unto men
- ❖ The work on the cross that defeated death, hell, and sin

During the Bible days, there were purpose-driven men and women of God who sought after God. In the Bible, people from all ethnic groups sought after God night and day throughout the Old Testament and the New Testament. The seekers in the Old and New Testaments are examples for believers today. Throughout their walk with God, they realized that there was a purpose behind seeking God. No matter what opposition stood in their way, these holy men and women made it a point to seek God to fulfill their purpose for being alive.

You, my brother and sister, must make or command your spirit, soul, and body to seek after the Holy Spirit to discover your purpose. The Holy Spirit makes it clear to some about their purpose, while others may not know their purpose right away. Twelve men forsook all and followed Jesus for three and a half years of service in order to receive the necessary training and equipping to take the gospel to the ends of the earth. Paul spent three years in the desert receiving knowledge, wisdom, and understanding from God that unlocked revelation, insight, strategies, solutions, principles, and commandments that would further the gospel throughout the earth (Galatians 1: 11 – 18). We are talking about the purpose behind seeking the Holy Ghost. Nehemiah discovered his purpose via seeking God. As a result of him seeking, he discovered a problem in Jerusalem and carried out a divine plan that allowed the walls of Jerusalem to be built in fifty-two days. (We won't even discuss the fact that Nehemiah and his people did not even go home, but chose to sleep, eat, and build next to the wall until it was completed.) Esther, along with the people of God, fasted, prayed, and went against the law. She also appeared before the king. The end result was that the Hebrew people were saved from genocide. Ruth stepped out on faith, forsook what she knew, entered the world of Jehovah, and was blessed with the "cream of the crop" in Boaz. Abraham left his family, city, and nation, and followed Jehovah Jirah. He is known as the father of natural and spiritual Israel.

What am I saying? These men and women of God were extraordinary seekers who discovered their God-given purpose through seeking the Father. They did not go one mile; they went the extra mile (Matthew 5:44). In order to figure out their purpose, these saints did not settle for the bare minimum in seeking God, but they went to the maximum in seeking Him.

David prayed to God seven times a day. He praised and worshipped God. He wrote songs and psalms unto God. He spent his mornings, afternoons, and evenings seeking God. When it was all said and done, he fulfilled his purpose by establishing a kingdom that was symbolic of the kingdom of God. The government was theocratic, order was in place, praise and worship took place twenty-four hours a day, the military conquered all enemies; and at death, his son was ready to inherit the kingdom.

Daniel fasted and prayed often. His purpose was fulfilled when he began to prophesy. He dreamed dreams and saw visions of biblical times and the future. Enoch walked with God for 300 years and eventually God took him (Genesis 5:21-24). Enoch's consistent and diligent seeking of God caused God to take him for Himself. Enoch's testimony was that he pleased God.

Seeking God is a foundational principle for every Christian. When you seek God, you will find Him and He will reveal your purpose to you, for God is the life source to all of humanity. If you do not plug into Him consistently, you will never find out your true purpose for existing. Seeking God unlocks the doors to your future.

Noah was a just and righteous man who sought after God. Eventually, his purpose was revealed to him. He preached righteousness to humanity for years and built an ark to save his family, himself, and two of every animal. Seeking God allows God to show you your purpose for being alive.

We also seek the Lord to have fellowship and communion with Him. The time spent with the Father should lead to a deeper, more intimate relationship with the Holy Spirit. In this relationship, we learn to be the Christ. In this relationship, we learn our true purpose in God. When each believer learns his or her purpose in God, then the body of Christ becomes more mature, more intelligent, more gifted, and more powerful. When we seek God and know our purpose, then the body of Christ will be in a better position to be effective witnesses in the world. Understand, Jesus came to save that which was lost. Once found, saved, and equipped, we become His ambassadors in the earth. As His representatives, we are responsible for nurturing, training, and equipping new converts.

Knowing our purpose comes via seeking the Father. This is why we seek. We do not seek God for ourselves, but we seek God for the person who will cross our path tomorrow, next week, or next month. Do you get my point? We seek God so that we can become the lifeline that reels in that sinner, the lost sheep, and the lukewarm believer. When we learn our purpose, we learn how we can give life to the people we encounter. This is what the art of seeking God is about. One has to make up in her mind that she is going to seek God and discover her purpose by any means necessary.

The key to seeking God is being obedient to what He tells you to do. God might tell you to do a specific thing. If He tells you to fast for two days, then fast for two days. If He tells you to study for sixty minutes, then study for sixty minutes. If He tells you to meditate every morning at 5:30am, then meditate every morning at 5:30am. The Spirit of God may exhort you to increase your daily prayer regimen. All you will want to do is pray. The Spirit of God might push you to read the Word. You might wonder why God wants you to do specific things devotionally or spontaneously. You never know whose path you might cross. Then, whatever God told you to do will make sense to you and be meaningful to the person you encounter.

One night while in all night prayer, I heard my sister in the Lord praying. As she was praying, she said, "Seek God like you seek out your paycheck. Seek God like you seek for a new job. Seek God like you seek out new relationships." The point is that we need to seek God like a thirsty person seeks water. We have to seek God like a hungry person seeks food. Seek God with passion. Seek God with enthusiasm. Seek God expecting to receive from Him. Seek God expecting Him to reveal Himself to you. We have to seek God until we know Him and until we know our purpose in the earth. God is the great I Am. We have to keep seeking Him because He will always have more of Himself to reveal to us. May you find your purpose in seeking God! Amen!

VALUABLE POINTS TO LIVE BY:

- ❖ Seeking God is a foundational principle for every Christian.
- ❖ Seeking God allows God to show you your purpose for being alive.
- ❖ As you seek God, be obedient to what He tells you to do.

"**S**eek My face until your face becomes My face."

Prophet Cornelius Hale

CHAPTER 4

SEEKING GOD EARLY

I Chronicles 16:11 states that we should seek the Lord's face continually. From reading the Word of God, it is clear that seeking God is mandatory for every believer in the Body of Christ. There are countless examples of God-fearing people who sought the face of God morning, noon, and night in the Bible. Not only did several God-fearing men and women seek God, they sought after God early in the morning. They were early seekers.

❖ In Genesis 22:3-5, Abraham rose up early to go worship the Lord on the mountain with his son Isaac.

❖ In Genesis 28:18, Jacob rose up early and built an altar unto God.

❖ In Exodus 34:4-29, Moses rose up early and went up on Mount Sinai to receive instructions from the Lord.

❖ In Judges 6:36-40, Gideon arose early in the morning to receive confirmation that at his hand he would deliver Israel.

❖ In 2 Chronicles 20:20, Jehoshaphat rose early in the morning exhorting the Israelites to believe in God, remain focused, believe on His prophets, and that they would prosper.

❖ In 2 Chronicles 29:20, Hezekiah rose early in the morning and went to the house of the Lord to offer sacrifices to the Lord.

❖ In Job 1:5, Job rose early to offer burnt offerings on behalf of his children.

❖ In Jeremiah 7:13, God makes mention time and time again of sending his prophets early to speak the Word of the Lord.

❖ In Jeremiah 25:3-4, Jeremiah reminded the people that for twenty-three years he spoke the word early and late to the Israelites.
❖ In Acts 5:20, the Apostles rose early and went to the temple declaring the whole doctrine centered on Christ.

Why does God command His sons and daughters to seek Him early in the morning? Why did these men and woman seek God early? What are the benefits to seeking God early? Why should one get out of bed at 4am, 5am, or 6am to seek God? Why can't one just wait until after work or later on in the day to seek God? There are several answers as to why we should seek God early.

For starters, let's look at Proverbs 8:17. The verse reads, "I love those that love me and those that seek me early shall find me." Those that seek God early will find Him. When you seek God early, you are going to find Him. The word *find* speaks of meeting God and discovering the secrets to your life and other meaningful things that pertain to the kingdom of God.

What does *early* speak of? Early speaks of several different things.

❖ Early speaks of the morning.
❖ Early speaks of a hunger and thirst to seek God as soon as possible each and every day.
❖ Early speaks of a race to get to God first. The early bird gets the worm.
❖ Early speaks of not wasting time.
❖ Early speaks of taking care of God's business first.
❖ Early speaks of getting to God before anyone else can get to you or before you can get to someone else.
❖ Early speaks of hearing from God first, before hearing from humans.
❖ Early speaks of persistence and diligence in a task.

God is calling us to arise early and to seek the kingdom of God before we seek our daily agendas. God is calling us to connect with Him early, before we connect with humanity. God is calling us to arise early and not waste time but be diligent about handling the Father's business.

When the children of Israel were in the wilderness, God sent them manna early in the morning (See Exodus, chapter 16). Manna was heavenly food the children of Israel had to gather in the morning before it went bad. The children of Israel were able to eat the manna throughout the day. The manna was only good for that one day. The next day, God sent new manna, fresh manna from heaven for the children of Israel to eat. The Bible states in John 1:1 and 1:14 in a summarized manner that, "In the beginning was the Word, and the Word was with God, and the Word was God, and the Word was made flesh and dwelt among us." The Bible goes on to say in John 6:33-35 that Jesus is the Bread of Heaven. The manna, the bread from heaven, is the Word of God. When we wake up each morning to eat the Word of God, to read the Word of God, we will receive knowledge, wisdom, and understanding that will give us life.

Each morning that we wake up, He is waiting to release spiritual manna into our lives. God releases spiritual manna via the Holy Ghost to those who arise early to gather it up. Let me be clear, if you make it a point to get up early every day and seek the Father, He has spiritual manna waiting for you to eat. I believe some of God's greatest words (revelations, insights, principles, etc.) are only being released to those who seek Him early. Strategies, directives, and methods that will allow you to grow, develop, solve problems, and prosper are being released early in the morning.

What happened to those who did not collect the manna in the morning? They did not receive the bread of heaven from God. When they went forth to collect the manna, it was gone until the next morning. Those people had to settle for quail, which is symbolic of a fleshly word that originated from the flesh realm. What if Christians all over the world decided to seek the Father first thing in the morning? I encourage you to set your alarm clock for some time between 4am – 6am to seek the Father. It is in the morning that God gives you fresh manna that will strengthen you, those in your household, those in your circle, and those to whom the Spirit of God directs you.

Isaiah 50:4 reads,

> "The Lord GOD hath given me the tongue of the
> learned, that I should know how to speak a word in
> season to him that is weary: <u>he wakeneth morning
> by morning, he wakeneth mine ear to hear as
> the learned.</u>"

God not only wakes up His servants in the morning, but He
wakes up His servant's ears to hear as the learned. The word *learned*
means discipled, accustomed to something; taught. The Spirit of
God is going to speak some things into your ears and allow you
to hear as a seasoned vessel. As a trained disciple, you are going
to hear some things that will allow you to grow, understand, and
mature in the things of God. What God speaks to you will train
you, equip you, teach you, and strengthen you for the journey that
is before you.

The Bible says in Matthew 10:16,

> "Behold I send you forth as sheep in the midst of
> wolves, therefore be wise as serpents and harmless
> as doves."

As Christians, we are compared to sheep. Most sheep have
shepherds who watch over them the same way our Shepherd
(John 10:11), Jesus Christ watches over us.

One of the jobs of a shepherd is to lead the sheep to water
that causes life to continue. Water is just as vital to sheep as it is
to humans. Without water, the sheep will die. This holds true for
humans also. Water allows sheep and humans to continue living.[1]
As Christians, we are described as sheep. Since we are described
as sheep, then we can look at the life of a sheep and discern principles about them that applies to us as Christians. Just like sheep,
Christians must drink water. The water that Christians drink is
just a little different. Christians drink the living water of Jesus
to ensure spiritual health and spiritual nutrition. If we go a little
deeper, in the animal kingdom, sheep drink the early morning

dew found on the grass. If the weather is not too hot, sheep can go for several weeks without actually drinking from a stream or pool. This is because as they graze in the early morning, the heavy dew supplies and satisfies their need for water. By nature's design, sheep will arise before dawn, or sometimes even during a full moon, and graze in the field both eating and drinking at the same time because of the dew (Gill).

As spiritual sheep, we are to arise by nature, early in the morning, and drink the Word of God and eat the Word of God. The water is symbolic of the Spirit of God. The food is the Word of God. When the two are mixed together, the Spirit of God brings life to the Word of God. The letter of the Word of God by itself kills (2 Cor. 3:6), or dries the spiritual body out, but the Spirit of the Word of God brings life and energy to the spiritual body which translate to the natural body. As Christians, we are to arise early and seek God morning by morning to receive our daily bread. In the early morning hours, you will receive that special attention that God wants you to have from Him.

Seeking God early is the key to a successful Christian life. Consistent early seeking will lead to a greater manifestation of God throughout your Christian life. Does that mean we as Christians shouldn't seek God at other times? God forbid! We should seek God when the opportunity presents itself. We should seek God in the morning, afternoon, and night.

Another reason to seek God early deals with priorities. God is the head of every believer's life. That means that He should get the first fruits of our day. Acknowledge Him first thing in the morning. He is our Father, our Leader, which means that we should check in with Him first to make sure we are taking and making the correct steps. He is the Groom and we, as His followers, are His bride. Common sense tells us that married folk should speak to each other first thing in the morning before the cares of this world begin to demand our attention.

Psalm 57:7- 8 reads,

"My heart is fixed, O God, my heart is fixed: I will sing and give praise. Awake up, my glory; awake, psaltery and harp: I myself will awake early."

David said he will wake up early; we must have the will and understanding that David had about seeking God early. The scripture stated that his heart was fixed on seeking God early. In other words, David's heart and mindset was firmly established on seeking God early. His heart was set up and directed to seek God. Just like David, we have to command our flesh to arise early and seek the face of God in prayer, praise, worship, etc. The popular phrase is that we should "awaken the dawn." Let's make it a point to consistently wake up before the day breaks to seek the face of God. He is waiting for you and me.

One morning while in meditation, the Lord said this to me, "Imagine yourself as a king over a great kingdom. Out of your kingdom, you have certain followers who wake up every morning to give you honor, praise, and worship. While they do that, the rest of your great servants lay in bed asleep. How would you feel towards these consistent early sunrise seekers?" Then He said, "You would want to bless them the more because of their sacrifice to you." Arise! Arise and seek God early! Amen!

VALUABLE POINTS TO LIVE BY:

- ❖ The word *find* speaks of meeting God and discovering the secrets to your life and other meaningful things that pertain to the kingdom of God.
- ❖ God is calling us to arise early and to seek the kingdom before we seek our daily agendas.
- ❖ When we wake up each morning to read (eat) the Word of God, we will receive knowledge, wisdom, revelation, insight, and understanding that will give us life.

"*If we seek God for our own good and profit, we are not seeking God.*"

Meister Eckhart

CHAPTER 5

BENEFITS TO
SEEKING GOD EARLY

I n this chapter, we are going to examine the various ways that one seeks God and the benefits that result from seeking God. Seeking God is likened unto working out at a fitness center. After working out at the gym consistently, you expect to see some results. The results may include muscle gain, loss of weight, more energy, and increased stamina. The same holds true for seeking God. After spending days, weeks, and months seeking God, you should see some positive results. The results may include:

- ❖ Being closer to God
- ❖ Being more knowledgeable of the Scriptures
- ❖ Having a deeper prayer life
- ❖ Having a holier lifestyle
- ❖ Use of spiritual gifts
- ❖ Godly character
- ❖ Receiving spiritual blessings
- ❖ Receiving natural blessings
- ❖ Being more prophetic
- ❖ Being more apostolic
- ❖ More supernatural power

The Bible states in Philippians 2:12, that we should, "…work out our own salvation with fear and trembling."

1 Timothy 4:8 goes on to state that, "…bodily exercise profiteth little: but godliness is profitable unto all things…"

Working out and bodily exercise requires labor or intense work that makes the body grow weary after the workout, but over time the body becomes strong and fit. Natural workouts provide natural gains that benefit one in this lifetime. Spiritual workouts provide spiritual and natural gains that benefit the believer in this life-time and the next one. Exercising your natural body has many benefits, but the profits or gains are little compared to godly exercising. Doing things that are godly is more profitable, advantageous, helpful, and beneficial than doing natural bodily exercises. A fit man or woman in the natural with their six-pack, chiseled arms, and defined back does not compare to a spiritually fit man or woman. The naturally fit man or woman can lift weights, run marathons, condition, and perform in the gym or on the field with the best of them. That naturally fit man or woman does not compare to a spiritually fit man or woman who can pray, hear God's voice, and execute biblical principles that convert sinners to productive saints.

The work put in as disciples of Christ should develop us into mature and productive sons of God. Below are eight benefits that result from you diligently seeking God. The greatest results will come when you seek God consistently and sincerely.

BENEFIT ONE
God Will Reward You for Seeking Him

The first benefit that I want to look at is found in Hebrews 11:6. The scripture reads, "But without faith it is impossible to please him: for he that cometh to God must believe that he is, and that he is a rewarder of them that diligently seek him." As Christians, we must first realize that we live by faith. Our lifestyle is wrapped up in one word: faith. We walk by faith, not by sight. Our whole life is centered on faith. Our lifestyle is not centered on moving from what we are able to see and comprehend. We are faith-based creatures who are led by the Spirit of God.

❖ Faith is moving forward based on a word spoken into your life, even though the manifestation of that word has not been seen or touched.
❖ Faith is believing that you are going to go to heaven, even though you have never seen heaven.
❖ Faith is believing that you are going to be healed from an incurable disease, even though the doctor has given you so many weeks to live.

❖ Faith is believing that you are going to buy the house, even though the mortgage banker is saying there's no way based off your credit score.

❖ Faith is speaking things that be not, as though they are.

When we seek God, we must believe that God is acting on our behalf. Operate by faith!

Another key word in the verse is *diligently* (steadfast, persistent, unrelenting). We must unrelentingly chase after God with all of our heart, soul, and mind. We must go after God hard. We must be consistent when we seek God. The prophet Elijah prayed for rain multiple times. He never lost faith when the rain didn't fall. Instead, he pressed into God even more via prayer. Eventually, an abundance of rain came pouring down. Elijah never lost the faith, but he diligently continued to seek God until the prayer was answered.

To summarize, if you don't have faith then you can't please God. If you have faith, you will believe in spite of your circumstances. Each time that God moves on your behalf, your faith will increase and get stronger. You will get closer to God and He will be closer to you. The end result of living by faith allows for spiritual and natural benefits to be released into your life. The rewards may be needs or wants. The rewards may include:

❖ Additional talents
❖ Improved character
❖ Better skills
❖ New gifts
❖ Financial increase
❖ Material things
❖ Healing
❖ Stronger walk with God
❖ Job promotion
❖ Innovative ideas
❖ New friendships
❖ Going to heaven

You will be rewarded when you live by and operate by faith.

BENEFIT TWO
You Will Experience God on a Greater Level

The second benefit is found in Matthew 7:7. The verse reads, "Ask, and it shall be given you; seek, and ye shall find; knock, and it shall be opened unto you." This entire verse deals with seeking God. The verse commands you to ask, seek, and knock. The result is that you will be exposed to a whole new level or dimension beyond the open door. The door is the "it". The "it" is anything that God wants you to encounter.

God wants you to ask. *Ask* means to beg, call for, crave, desire, and require. You are the lesser creature petitioning the Creator to meet the need of what you are asking for. The need or want will be supplied according to the will of God for your life. When you live a life of worship, you are endeavoring or seeking to be one with the Father. When you are one with the Father, then you will begin to operate in the authority, dominion, and power of the kingdom. When you are asking, you are seeking God on the thirty-fold level. This is level one seeking. The benefit to this level of seeking is that, when you ask, you will receive from God. He will hear the petition and you will receive the answer. The answer may range from natural things to spiritual things.

God wants you to seek Him. *Seek* means to endeavor, worship, and desire. We have to desire to live a lifestyle of worship. We should continuously seek to perfect our lifestyle until we come into the fullness of God. Understand that when you seek after God, it's equivalent to trying to find someone or something. When you seek for something or someone, you have to prepare your mind to explore common and odd spots. When you are seeking for something or someone, you hope that it is a quick find. With this level of seeking, there may be some stress when it comes to seeking after God. Regardless of how long you are seeking, you must keep the faith and believe that you will find the One that you are seeking. As we seek the Father, we will find Him. Once we find Him, He will answer our prayers and start revealing things to us. The things that He reveals to you will be about you, your family, friends, enemies, and other things that pertain to your life. This is the sixty-fold level of seeking.

God wants you to knock. This is the third level of seeking, hundred-fold seeking. *Knock* means to rap or strike. One knocks on a door because he or she wants to enter a specific building, room, and/or dimension. When we knock on the door to seek the Father, it is because we want a face-to-face with Him. Jesus said, knock and the door shall be opened. What is the door speaking of? The door is speaking of a divine opening that only God can open or shut. In the process of consistent knocking, eventually a door will open that has on the other side your true purpose for life. The door that will be opened will lead to your true spiritual purpose that will manifest in the natural. The fact of the matter is that unrelenting knocks on a door always leads to someone answering and opening the door. We know that God wants to open the doors to our future, so let us keep knocking until the door is opened.

An example of an asking, seeking, and knocking prayer would be Jesus in the garden of Gethsemane. Read Matthew 26: 36-46 and Luke 22: 39 – 46. Jesus prayed three times and each time he prayed harder and harder. The last level of prayer and the stress involved was so real that He began to sweat great drops of blood. Jesus had the faith and He accepted the Father's will. He put the work in when He went to the cross. The asking, seeking, and knocking led Jesus to fulfilling His purpose by conquering sin, death, and hell. What looked like defeat turned into victory when the resurrection of Jesus took place. We as believers benefit from asking, seeking, and knocking because the Father reveals our God-given purpose. When we walk in our God-given purpose other benefits may or may not result from seeking the Father. Let's make it a point to seek the Father via asking, seeking, and knocking.

BENEFIT THREE
When You Seek, All Things Will Be Added to Your Life

The third benefit is found in Matthew 6:33. The scriptures reads, "But seek ye first the kingdom of God, and his righteousness; and all these things shall be added unto you." The command is to seek the kingdom of God and His righteousness *first*. *His righteousness* is referring to the integrity and virtue of Jesus. Righteousness refers to the purity of the life of Jesus, His correctness of thinking, feeling, and acting. The kingdom speaks of doing things God's way here on Earth. The kingdom speaks of bringing what's in heaven (love, order, power, healing, peace, etc.) to the Earth realm.

We should seek the kingdom of God in the morning consistently. Our main J-O-B on this Earth is to seek the kingdom of God. When we seek the kingdom of God first, then we unlock the doors to our present and future. Once we get it in our spirit, soul, and body to seek the kingdom first, then we will realize that our spiritual and natural needs and wants are being met, and will be met according to God's timeline for our lives.

When we truly begin to seek the kingdom of God, then we will begin to tap into the strategies, methods, and tactics of God that will bring healing to self, family, friends, communities, and nations. Then we can take what God has shown us and apply it to our daily lives. Consistent kingdom seeking leads to a deeper relationship with Jesus. Once we can relate to the Spirit of God and operate with the mind of Christ, then and only then can we become productive citizens in the kingdom.

Seeking the kingdom of God is a benefit because you can find what your niche is in the kingdom of God. Every joint must supply (Ephesians 4:16). Once you know your role in the kingdom of heaven, you can begin to set up shop or build a foundation in that department that God has for you. The main goal is not material gain but spiritual maturity that is truly focused on the will of God for establishing the kingdom of God.

BENEFIT FOUR
Healing of the Land

An individual and corporate benefit to seeking God is found in 2 Chronicles 7:14. The scripture reads, "If my people, which are called by my name, shall humble themselves, and pray, and seek my face, and turn from their wicked ways; then will I hear from heaven, and will forgive their sin, and will heal their land." This will bless humanity. It not only involves seeking the face of God, but it also calls for all believers to humble themselves, pray, and repent.

We live in a terrible time where all kinds of atrocities are taking place every day. In countries all across the world, divorce, sexual perversion, sickness, rape, trafficking, murder, and stealing are taking place at an all-time high. We need God to heal the land, and it starts with the people of God. While this precious benefit might not include material gain and finances, it does benefit God's people along with their family and friends because God turns His attention towards us. The enemy is forever tempting, persecuting, and causing tribulation for the people of God. The onslaught of the enemy has left parts of the body of Christ in a lukewarm and cold state that has allowed fleshly desires to birth lust that has led to sin and even death for some. Sin leads to curses, and curses bring decay and ruin to the people of God. *What affects God's people directly affects the rest of the world indirectly.*

The drawback of God's people not seeking Him leads to a world that becomes more infested with devils that demonize, terrorize, manipulate, deceive, oppress, and even possess the people of this world. We, as God's people, can no longer sit on the sidelines as spectators and allow the world to go into further ruin and decay. Now is the time to seek the face of God. Now is the time to humble ourselves. *Humble* means to submit to the Word of God, the ways of God, and the will of God with total obedience. Now is the time to pray to God. Prayer is simply talking to God (see Appendix A). Now is the time to seek God. Now is the time to turn from our wicked ways. Turning from our wicked ways has to deal with repentance and changing our mind. If we truly change our mind, then we will change our daily conduct. When we seek the Father in the above way, then God will hear, forgive, and heal. He will hear our prayers, forgive our sins, and heal individuals, families, communities, states, and nations. As we seek God individually and corporately, then all of humanity will benefit from natural and spiritual healing.

BENEFIT FIVE
No Lack

When you seek God, you will not lack any good thing. Psalm 34:10 reads,

> "The young lions do lack, and suffer hunger: but they that seek the LORD shall not want any good thing."

Seeking God is never in vain, and even though there are benefits connected to seeking God, we should never have the mentality that one seeks God to get. God is not a genie who just gives us what we want when we want it. The focus should be seeking God to get to know Him in order to live a kingdom lifestyle. Understand that as you seek God, He is still going to bless you. In this scripture, the end result is that you will not want any good thing. The word "want" means to lack or be without. When we seek God, we will not lack any good thing. In other words, when you seek God, you are going to get some things. The things could be in the natural or they could be in the spiritual. The things could be wants or they could be needs. Whatever the thing is, it will be good and it will be in line with God's will for your life. Seek God and expect to receive some gifts, talents, skills, and virtues. Seek the Father and watch Him add to your life in the natural and the spiritual.

BENEFIT SIX
Understanding Comes via Seeking God

Proverbs 28:5 states,

> "Evil men understand not judgment: but they that seek the LORD understand all things."

The benefit is that when you seek God you will understand all things. Seeking God allows you to be in tune with the Spirit of God. When you get in tune with the Holy Spirit you will begin to pick up on spiritual intelligence that is going across the airwaves. The Bible states in I Corinthians 2:15 that, "…he that is spiritual judgeth all things." When we as believers understand all things then we can make proper judgements when dealing with the affairs of mankind. It is important that we seek God because having understanding about natural and spiritual things is key to making an impact in our communities. Seek God consistently and watch Him increase your understanding in all things.

BENEFIT SEVEN
Seek and You Will Live

Another beautiful benefit that comes from seeking God is found in Amos 5:4. It reads, "For thus saith the LORD unto the house of Israel, Seek ye me, and ye shall live:" God is telling His people, if they just seek Him, they will live. From this verse and others, we understand that seeking God includes more than just completing or doing different disciplines like prayer, reading, and studying. Seeking involves putting in some actions that lead to life. The actions involve putting our trust in God, obeying His Word, and being led by the Holy Spirit. In the verse, the word *live* is talking about being repaired, restored, and preserved.

When one seeks after God, He can save you from the harsh consequences on this earth and hell in the life to come. God is making it plain to us that if we just seek Him then we will live.

Mark 10:29-31 reads,

> "And Jesus answered and said, Verily I say unto you, There is no man that hath left house, or brethren, or sisters, or father, or mother, or wife, or children, or lands, for my sake, and the gospel's, But he shall receive an hundredfold now in this time, houses, and brethren, and sisters, and mothers, and children, and lands, with persecutions; and in the world to come eternal life. But many that are first shall be last; and the last first."

Seek God and live! No matter what you may gain on this earth in the natural and the spiritual, just know that the greatest gift that we can receive when we seek after God is eternal life. One day this world will come to an end, and just having the reassurance that life in heaven belongs to those that seek God's face is amazing.

BENEFIT EIGHT
Developing a Relationship with Jesus Christ

The greatest benefit to seeking God is that you will develop a relationship with Jesus Christ. You will move past the surface and into the deeper things of God. Seeking God will allow you to move from the outer court, to the inner court, and all the way into the Holy of Holies. The deeper the relationship means the more real God will be in your life. Developing a relationship with God should be the goal of every Christian. As you seek and develop a relationship with the Father, keep one thing in mind: God's thoughts are not our thoughts and God's ways are not our ways. As the heavens are above the earth so are God's thoughts and ways above our thoughts and ways. So be open, sensitive, and most of all obedient to the Spirit of God and you will have an intimate relationship with the Father that is built on love.

SUMMARY OF BENEFITS FROM SEEKING GOD:

1. God will reward you for seeking Him
2. You will experience God on a greater level.
3. When you seek God, all things will be added to your life.
4. God will heal the land.
5. You will not experience spiritual or natural lack in your life.
6. God will increase your understanding when you seek God.
7. Seeking God will allow you to live in this life, and especially the next life.
8. You will develop a relationship with God.

"**A**rt is coming face to face with yourself."

Jackson Pollock

"**Y**ou will find what you seek."

Lailah Gifty Akita

CHAPTER 6

In Spite Of, Don't Stop Seeking

In Galatians 6:7-9 it reads,

> "Be not deceived; God is not mocked: for whatsoever a man soweth, that shall he also reap. For he that soweth to his flesh shall of the flesh reap corruption; but he that soweth to the Spirit shall of the Spirit reap life everlasting. And let us not be weary in well doing: for in due season we shall reap, if we faint not."

The Bible is decorated with men and woman of God who were serious about seeking the Father. These men and women of God did not allow people or situations to stop them from seeking God and fulfilling His purpose. The apostles come to mind in the book of Acts. On a few different occasions, the Pharisees and Sadducees tried their best to shut down the apostles from preaching the kingdom of God, but it did not work. It did not matter if the apostles were locked up in jail, beaten, shipwrecked, or threatened, they did not stop seeking after God. Paul and Silas were seeking the face of God at midnight while they were locked up in prison and God showed up. The people of God were praying, and an angel released Peter from prison. Paul was so close to God that even when he got bitten by a viper, the poison could not harm him. We, like the apostles in the book of Acts, have to be so focused on seeking God that nothing hinders us from seeking God. When Paul got saved there were still rumors going around that he was trying to kill Christians, but that did not stop Paul from seeking God and fulfilling his purpose. It was at Ziklag that David had to encourage himself in the Lord because his own men wanted to kill him. Nehemiah, Daniel, the three Hebrew boys (Shadrach, Meshach, and Abednego), and other God-fearing people in the Bible provide great examples of saints who did not lose their seek regardless of the obstacles that they faced. In spite of the difficulty that biblical characters encountered, they stayed true to seeking God. When they were faced with frustration, hunger, persecution, and opposition, they continued to seek after God.

They never gave up, and they never gave in to persecution, temptations, or the trials of life. Just like us, I am sure that they had to deal with all kinds of mental warfare. The enemy probably did his best to make them quit the race that we call salvation. I am sure that the apostles in the book of Acts had to deal with all kinds of emotions daily and weekly that attacked their belief system, faith, confidence, boldness, and kingdom principles. These holy men and women of God in the Bible were true examples to us. Paul said it best in 2 Corinthians 4:8-9, "We are troubled on every side, yet not distressed; we are perplexed, but not in despair; Persecuted, but not forsaken; cast down, but not destroyed;" They were focused, fixated, and driven on seeking God and fulfilling their purpose in God.

I remember an earlier time in my walk with God when I was studying the Word of God. I was so frustrated because I was studying faithfully, but my understanding was unfruitful. My study notes were atrocious. I was starting to feel defeated when I was studying. The way I was trying to break the Word of God down did not make sense. This went on for days, weeks, and months. Then one night while I was studying, out of nowhere, I felt the Holy Ghost come alive on the inside of me and my understanding of the scriptures began to increase. What I was writing down was revelatory. The scriptures that I was reading became clear and meaningful to my life. The Holy Ghost was teaching me as I sat in my chair studying. I went from feeling frustrated to feeling overjoyed because the Holy Ghost was teaching me the Word of God. There were times when I was seeking God in prayer, praise, and worship and I did not feel anything or sense anything, but I did not stop seeking.

When you begin to seek God and you feel like you are not getting the results that you want, you have to keep pushing yourself. No one becomes great at seeking God overnight. To become great at something you have to put work in consistently. You have to work hard! Understand, God is not a genie. You can't do a trick formula to make Him appear. He is God! Like the saying goes, "He might not show up when you want Him to, but He always shows up right on time." Our job is to seek God until we find Him or until He reveals Himself to us.

Throughout my Christian walk I have crossed paths with many family members, friends, and associates who were totally against the things of God. They made that clear to me via their words and actions. There were those who belittled me with their words. Others made fun of me for being a Christian. Regardless of who proved to be an enemy directly or indirectly, I refused to stop and will refuse to stop seeking God and running the race that Paul spoke of in the Holy Scriptures (2 Timothy 4:7). I will seek God and I will fulfil my God-given purpose.

In life, you are going to have questions. Things are not always going to make sense. There are times when you are going to be in some uncomfortable situations. You will feel like your whole life is being turned upside down. It is in moments like these that you have to seek God. No matter what life throws your way, keep seeking God. Do not let your thoughts side-track you from seeking God. The devil will do everything within his power to stop you from seeking God. Everything in your life could be great in the natural and the spiritual. Then, out of nowhere, things begin to happen to shake up your whole life. Think about the life of Job. His body was attacked by sickness and he lost just about everything, but he did not stop seeking God.

The best thing to do is to set aside time that is devoted to seeking God. Trust me, it will not be easy, because life has a way of interfering with our plans. Life sends all kinds of things our way to stop us from seeking God. Death, life, weddings, marriage, kids, jobs, material things, positive things, negative things, and a whole lot more will hit our lives at different times. Just know that when these things come our way, we have to be ready mentally and spiritually to keep seeking God. The Bible states in Romans 8:38-39, "For I am persuaded, that neither death, nor life, nor angels, nor principalities, nor powers, nor things present, nor things to come, Nor height, nor depth, nor any other creature, shall be able to separate us from the love of God, which is in Christ Jesus our Lord." When life comes to hinder and stop your seek, you have to motivate and push yourself to keep seeking God.

I encourage you, my brother and my sister, to seek God in spite of what comes your way. Remember, life is full of mountain top experiences and valley experiences. There are going to be some days and nights that you are super excited about life and other days and nights when you are in a gloomy and dejected mood. In spite of your situation, be it high or low, you and I have to seek the face of God.

VALUABLE POINTS TO LIVE BY:

- ❖ We, like the apostles in the book of Acts, have to be so focused on seeking God that nothing hinders us from seeking God.
- ❖ Like the apostles, we have to be focused, fixated, and driven to seek God and fulfill our purpose in God.
- ❖ When life comes to hinder and stop your seek, you have to motivate and push yourself to keep seeking God.

"**H**ow strong is your desire to know the Savior?"

Lailah Gifty Akita

CHAPTER 7

DRAWBACKS OF NOT
SEEKING GOD

The Bible plainly states that if you seek God you will find Him and live (Amos 5:4). The Bible also makes it clear that if you forsake Him, He will forsake you. Psalm 9:17 states that we should seek Him while He may be found. That means a day is coming when those who fail to seek God will seek Him and not be able to find Him. There are great benefits to seeking God, but there are grave consequences for those who do not seek God. God said He would not strive with man always. He said His hand is still stretched out for those who want Him (Isaiah 5:25; 9:12, 17; 10:14).

Not seeking God is like not eating natural food or drinking water. Slowly but surely, your body is going to begin to wither away. Then, eventually, you are going to die. The same holds true for seeking God. If you do not seek God, not only will you die naturally, but you will also die spiritually. Millions of Christians are on spiritual life support and they don't even know it. The plug could be pulled at any time. Failure to seek God will cause you to fall into the hands of the devil. The trap the devil lays out for you will eventually cause you to die when your space of grace runs out. God said in His Word that He wishes for no one to perish, but for all to have life (2 Peter 3:9). There were people who denied and rejected Jesus, but He still wanted them saved. He said He did not come to destroy man but to save man. He said that He came to give life and life more abundantly (John 10:10).

I urge you brothers and sisters to seek God consistently, for your eternal life is in the seeking. All God wants from you is a relationship with Him. He seeks to be your God, Father, Friend, Companion, Comforter, Counselor, and so much more. God wants you badly! The problem is that many do not want God in the same way that He wants them. Not seeking God is the same as rejecting Him. You might like Him and love Him, but you do not *want* Him. It's like you just want to have a one-night stand with God versus a lifetime commitment. Some think God is a "get out of trouble" card. When you do not seek God, it affects you, your household, your place of employment, the House of God, and whatever else is around you. Jesus is the Way, the Truth, and the Life, no human gets to God but via Jesus (John 14:6). So, when you refuse to seek God you go the wrong way and you hear truth mixed with 99% of deception. You blindly walk the path of death. Death is wrapped up in deception, and death does not lead to truth. As a result, you blindly walk into death and not life. If you choose to not seek God, you bring an environment of death around you and all those around you.

Here is an example. There is a family of four (father, mother, son, and daughter). This household does not believe in God. He is a doctor and she is a housewife. They have instilled in their children good morals (do good to all people, abstinence from sex, "Just Say No" to drugs and alcohol, honesty, integrity, righteousness). We have a whole family full of good morals, but they shun the idea of salvation through Jesus Christ's death, burial, and resurrection and everything that has to do with the life of a believer. They believe in man, science, technology, and information. They believe in and seek after the American dream—life, liberty and the pursuit of happiness. This outlook they have on life has been passed down from generation to generation in their family. This is a family that has been conformed to the world. In the world, there are many cultures that people seek to live out, but those cultures are opposed to God's culture.

In this region of the world, America, the above family is seeking to become all they can be from an American point of view. They want life, liberty, and the pursuit of happiness, but not according to God's standards. What is their condition? They are alive, yet dead; they are awake, yet sleep. They are the walking dead. They want the best for humanity, but they fail to realize that the best for humanity is the will of God and not the will of man. Unless something gives in their lives, they will all be guilty of rejecting God instead of seeking God. Their moral, driven family lives in an environment of death because they have chosen to go another way full of deceit that leads to death and not life. There are millions of people who are heading to hell for simply rejecting Jesus Christ.

When you choose not to seek God, it is the same as putting fish (humans) into a tank (the world) full of piranhas (demons). The fish will live for a while, but eventually grace and mercy will run out and those fish will be devoured by the piranhas. The same holds true for humans who do not seek God. Eventually, you will be destroyed. If you don't seek God, you seek death and you don't even know it. It is like receiving a present wrapped in beautiful wrapping paper with a golden bow. The present looks good on the outside but when you open it—DEATH.

Understand that Satan has a five-fold ministry of his own. He wants to seek you, sift you, steal your dreams, kill your purpose, and destroy you. I Peter 5:8 reads, "Be sober, be vigilant; because your adversary the devil, as a roaring lion, walketh about, seeking whom he may devour." The devil and his evil host are seeking to destroy the saints of God. That word *devour* means to gulp down entirely, swallow up, and/or destroy. Once he finds you, he will sift you. Luke 22:31 states, "And the Lord said, Simon, Simon, behold, Satan hath desired to have you, that he may sift you as wheat." The word *sift* means to shake, to examine closely, investigate, or to try. Taking the word sift deeper, it means to shake by inward agitation and to try one's faith to the verge of overthrow. Sift means to agitate, to excite or disturb emotionally. In the Bible, the natural sifting process meant that the wheat was left in a fan and shaken or agitated. The shaking of the wheat separated the grain from the chaff or husk/dust. The grain was kept, and the chaff or dust was blown away or thrown out. For believers there is also a spiritual sifting process.

You and I will experience a spiritual shaking (sifting) in our lives from time to time. The spiritual shaking is when we face great temptations or great situations that come to agitate us or to shake us. The sifting that the enemy sends our way will show what is in us, faith or faithlessness; godliness or ungodliness; righteousness or unrighteousness. Once the devil sees that you are shaken and not the man or woman of God that you claim to be, he moves in for the steal and the kill. He wants steal your dreams and kill your purpose. His end game is to see your entire life destroyed in the natural and the spiritual. It is imperative that we seek the face of God consistently. I encourage you to seek the Father to avoid the consequences that are coming to those who do not seek God. Accepting Jesus Christ into your life and seeking His face is the greatest thing that you can do on this earth.

VALUABLE POINTS TO LIVE BY:

- ❖ There are great benefits to seeking God but there are grave consequences for those who do not seek God.
- ❖ I urge you brothers and sisters to seek God consistently, for your eternal life is in the seeking.

"Those who seek should not stop seeking until they find. When they find, they will be disturbed. When they are disturbed, they will marvel, and will rule over all."

Gospel of Thomas

CHAPTER 8

THE GREATEST SEEKER

The daily life of Jesus Christ shows those from the past, present, and future how a seeker is to seek the Father. Scripture makes it clear that Jesus Christ consistently sought after the Father. He was relentless, dedicated, passionate, and intentional about spending time with the Father. This chapter will showcase Jesus seeking the Father.

In one of the earliest biblical accounts of Jesus, we find His parents, Mary and Joseph, frantically searching for Him (Read Luke 2:42-51). He came up missing and His parents looked for Him and could not find Him. When they did find Him, He was in the temple with the spiritual leaders asking questions and answering questions. His 'God IQ' was so on point that the rabbis and priests He was working with were confounded. Once found and questioned by His mother, His response is the seedbed for those in the faith. He said, "How is it that ye sought me? Wist ye not that I must be about my Father's business?" From this question alone we can glean that this was not this 12-year old's first time having a God encounter.

Someone put it in His head that there is a God, the Father, and that He was His Son. From a young age, Jesus understood that He had to seek the Father. We can infer that at some point before the age of twelve, Jesus was focused on seeking God. He wanted to become an intelligent man of God who knew the Father from A to Z and then some. We do not know for certain at what age He began to seek God, but He knew about the temple and the priests. He knew that the priests were discussing information pertinent to His development as a man of God. Not only that, but He understood that the temple was the breeding ground for the sons of God. Before He made the trip to the temple, He knew that the prerequisite was seeking the Father. To be able to go into the temple and have an adult conversation with educated men of God means that young Jesus spent some time with the Father. His parents, including His Father in heaven, must have trained Him on how to read, how to study, how to meditate, how to ask the right questions, and how to approach God in prayer.

By age twelve, Jesus had a hunger and a thirst for the things of God that played a part in His development when He came on the scene eighteen years later at age thirty. Before He was baptized, He knew the importance of prayer. Before He was identified as the Son of God, He had the discipline to steal away and seek the Father. All the seeking that Jesus did before age twelve lead to the moment where He was able to dialogue in the most intelligent manner with the rabbis. All the seeking that He did prior to age thirty led to the moment when He said, "Repent, the Kingdom of Heaven is at hand." Then from age thirty until the time that He ascended up to the right hand of God, He sought God in a consistent manner. Scripture gives us several accounts of how Jesus sought His Heavenly Father.

Luke 5:15-16 reads,

> "But so much the more went there a fame abroad
> of him: and great multitudes came together to hear,
> and to be healed by him of their infirmities. And he
> withdrew himself into the wilderness, and prayed."

During this time in His life, Jesus was a household name. The text says that great multitudes came to hear Him and be healed by Him. He was known and people sought Him out. There was a major demand on His life. Jesus preached and taught the Word of God with authority. He left multitudes astonished and amazed at how God used Him to heal the sick, cast out devils, and raise the dead. Even with the major demand on His life, He knew how to separate Himself from the masses. In the above text, we see Him withdrawing Himself into the wilderness. The wilderness is a lonely place, but it is also the place where one can spend quality time with God. Jesus had the discipline to stop what He was doing and go pray. Prayer is simply talking to God. We know that from scripture Jesus spent His time always referring back to the Father. If the Father did not endorse what He was doing, then He didn't do it; but if His Father backed it, then He was quick to execute the things of God.

The only way that He would truly know what the Father wanted was by spending time with the Father in prayer. Praying is what we witness Jesus doing in verse 15. Prayer birthed everything in the life of Jesus, and prayer is going to birth everything in our lives. If something godly took place in the Word of God, then it was birthed in prayer. Jesus was not afraid to be alone and He was not afraid to be with the Father. Just like Jesus, we have to be willing to withdraw to the wilderness and pray. In the Bible, there were men of God who withdrew themselves, prayed, and received detailed instructions from God. If you are going to seek God, then you have to be willing to withdraw yourself and seek the Father in prayer.

Luke 6:11-12 reads,

> "And they were filled with madness; and communed one with another what they might do to Jesus. And it came to pass in those days, that he went out into a mountain to pray, and continued all night in prayer to God."

Here we find Jesus going to a mountain to pray to God all night. According to scriptures, mountains are significant places where natural men meet the supernatural God. Mountains are known as the place of God (Moses and the Ten Commandments – Read Exodus chapters 19 and 20). Mountains are where God's miracles took place (Moses with his raised hands – Read Exodus 17: 8 –16). Mountains are where supernatural activity takes place (The transfiguration of Jesus – Matthew 17: 1 – 9). It is not surprising that Jesus spent all night in prayer to the Father on a mountain. The next day, He handpicked His twelve disciples. I believe at some point during the all-night prayer session, the Father began to speak to His Son about the team that was about to be assembled. Jesus prayed all night. *All night* means that He was in prayer anywhere from six to twelve hours. I do not know if He prayed for several hours straight or if His all-night prayer session included prayer, meditation, praise, worship, and singing.

I got saved on February 11, 1996. Over the years, I have witnessed and experienced many different versions of what all night prayer entails. All night prayer for you or the church you attend may include some of the items from the above, but may include several people taking a lead role during the all-night prayer session. The all-night prayer may include you praying alone, in a group, or corporately. The all-night prayer sessions may be super organized with structure, or it may be a Spirit-led prayer session. The main point here is that Jesus was seeking His Heavenly Father all night in prayer.

What is the purpose of all-night prayer? All-night prayer will position you to hear from God with clarity about natural and spiritual matters. All-night prayer will allow you to pray on important topics thoroughly. Seeking God in all-night prayer allows for the one praying to receive clarity and direction about specific topics.

Luke 9:18 reads,

> "And it came to pass, as he was alone praying, his disciples were with him: and he asked them, saying, Whom say the people that I am?"

Here is another time where we find Jesus seeking His Father. He is alone and He is praying. Jesus shows us a pattern of consistently seeking His Father in prayer. The beauty of His prayers always led to a profound revelation or the establishment of something that would set the tone for the Christian walk. The answer to the question led to the revelation that Jesus was not just your normal prophet, but that He was, and is, the Son of God, the Christ of God. The Christ of God, interpreted, means that Jesus is the Anointed of God. It is as if, while in prayer, the Father downloaded the Son with a statement, a question, or a directive that further established Him as the Son of God, the Lord of Lords, and God in the flesh. The point is that while in prayer, while seeking the Father, if you pray with your words and listen with your spiritual ears then you will hear what the Father is speaking to you, your family, your city, and even the nations. What He gives you will have a profound IMPACT on your life.

Luke 11:1 reads,

> "And it came to pass, that, as he was praying in a certain place, when he ceased, one of his disciples said unto him, Lord, teach us to pray, as John also taught his disciples."

When it comes to seeking God, some things have to be taught. In the verse, the disciples are asking Jesus to teach them how to pray. He makes it clear to His disciples that when one prays, he/she is asking, seeking, and knocking. These are three levels of prayer. Asking is the first level of prayer. Seeking is the second level of prayer. Knocking is the third level of prayer. I Kings, chapter 18, demonstrates the prophet Elijah praying these three types of prayer. The Word of the Lord stated that God would send rain. The Bible says that Elijah prayed seven times. During the first level, Elijah asked the Lord to send the rain and no rain came. In between prayers, he sent his servant to check to see if the rain was in sight. The servant reported that there was no rain in sight. Elijah prayed again. His prayer grew a little more intense. I can hear Elijah praying, "God, I know You said You were going to send the rain. I prayed and the rain did not come. Now I am asking You again to send the rain." The rain still did not fall. His asking now shifted from asking to seeking. During this second level of prayer, Elijah begins to seek after God in prayer. He is now praying for the fourth and fifth time. With more passion, he takes his prayer to another level, believing that God is about to send the rain. As he is seeking God in prayer, Elijah is now praying in a manner to pinpoint the God of heaven. He is seeking and trying to locate Jehovah. Even with the increased prayer, God did not send the rain. Then, during the sixth prayer session and especially the seventh prayer session, Elijah began to get more forceful with his prayer. He began to knock on the doors of heaven, beat or even strike the doors of heaven. This is the third level of prayer. Whatever he prayed that seventh time literally got God's attention. The Lord sent the rain. During this third level of prayer, Elijah did not take anything for granted. He prayed until he prayed. He pressed in to prayer until the word of the Lord that was spoken to him came to pass.

Now, let's dig a little deeper. With his mind, Elijah was asking or making a request to God for the rain to be sent. Then, he shifted to seeking God in a deeper manner. With his whole heart, he was questioning, reasoning, meditating, and demanding God to send the rain. After asking with his mind and seeking God with his heart, he decided to knock on the doors of heaven. Knocking on the doors of heaven is when you pray to God with your mind and heart in complete agreement. Knocking on the doors of heaven is the level of prayer where you are locked in on God. You feel Him and He feels you. When you knock on the doors of heaven you are like the man in Luke 11:8. That man did not care about the hour of the night. He did not care who he was disturbing. He knew what he wanted, and because he had no shame, his friend ended up giving him what he wanted.

My friend, when you pray, don't give up and don't give in, but pray until something happens. Be like Jesus and pray like a PRO! Be persistent in prayer. Be relentless in prayer. Be obsessed in prayer. The Bible says, ask and you shall receive, seek and ye shall find, and knock and the doors shall be opened. Sometimes, your asking will get God's attention. Sometimes your seeking will get God's attention. At other times, knocking will get God's attention. When you ask God, you make a request. When you ask, you are hoping for a quick answer or response. When you ask God, there's no rhyme or reason. You ask and you expect to receive. This level of prayer is less stressful than the other levels of prayer. This is thirty-fold prayer. Seeking is sixty-fold prayer. Seeking is when you are looking for someone or something. You are prepared to explore. You will look in the common and uncommon spots. When you seek, you are hoping to find Him quickly. You are not planning on seeking for too long. You believe you will find what you are seeking. This level of prayer has an increased level of stress. Knocking on the doors of heaven is one hundred-fold praying. You want the door to be opened so that you can enter in to commune with the Father. When you knock, you want to see the Father face-to-face. You want to see how He gets down. You want to see how He is living. You want Him to know that it is serious. This is the highest level of stress. This is when you are face-to-face with the Father, and though the answer is delayed, you continue to press in until God answers your prayer.

When Esther prayed and fasted, there was a high level of stress associated with those prayers. She knew that going before the king without permission might cost her, her life, but her faith saved a nation. When you and I are praying for a loved one who is facing a serious illness, or when a loved one is passing from this side of heaven to the other, there is a high level of stress. Jesus raised the bar when it came to seeking the Father.

Mark 1:35 reads,

> "And in the morning, rising up a great while before day, he went out, and departed into a solitary place, and there prayed."

The Greatest Seeker, Jesus Christ, sought His Father in prayer early in the morning. Not only that, but He sought the Father in a solitary place. He purposed to meet God in prayer while everyone was still sleeping. He sought God void of distractions. He got up and left the confines of comfort and went to seek God in an uncomfortable place. When you start out seeking God in prayer and meditation it may seem uncomfortable, scary or even pointless. You may spend your time in that solitary place praying to God and you might not hear Him. You might not feel Him. You might not understand. You might be tired and weary, but when God shows up everything changes.

What seems to be an uncomfortable place will literally become comfortable because the Holy Spirit will meet you in that place. From day to day and week to week the uncomfortable place becomes a comfortable place. It will get to a place that, even before you get there, the Father is already talking with you. Jesus woke up early and went to that solitary place to commune with the

Father. It's in the solitary place that you learn to hear and feel the heartbeat of God. It's in the solitary place where God can strip you, teach you, prepare you, and equip you to be a servant leader.

Luke 4:1 and Luke 4:14 read,

> "And Jesus being full of the Holy Ghost returned from Jordan, and was led by the Spirit into the wilderness, And Jesus returned in the power of the Spirit into Galilee: and there went out a fame of him throughout all the region round about."

In the verses above, Jesus was full of the Holy Ghost and was led by the Spirit into the wilderness. When He left the wilderness forty days later, the Bible says that He returned in the power of the Spirit. After seeking God for forty days and forty nights in prayer and fasting, He was fully empowered by the Spirit of God. He came back to Galilee and the other cities and did major ministry that shook the heavens and the earth. The way Jesus sought the Father is the way we should seek the Father. Just like Jesus, we have to discipline ourselves to seek the Father. Seeking the Father allows Him to download you, impart into you, and leave deposits in you. When you seek the Father, He will take out of you what should not be there and deposit into you what you need to grow and develop into a mighty man or woman of God. Seeking God consistently and habitually will take you from being led by the Spirit of God to being empowered by the Spirit of God.

All in all, Jesus Christ spent time with the Father. He sought His Father all throughout the day and night in different manners. He made Himself available to the Father. In return, the Father revealed Himself to Jesus. Jesus did not take the Father for granted. Jesus knew who He was, but He still sought after God. He knew that seeking God face-to-face would empower Him by the Spirit of God to teach with authority, preach with passion, heal the sick, cast out devils, raise the dead, perform miracles, signs, wonders, and mighty deeds. What Jesus did in word and deed, you and I can also do. Put the work in, seek the Father, and watch Him empower you to change the world around you.

VALUABLE POINTS TO LIVE BY:

- ❖ If something godly took place in the Word of God, then it was birthed in prayer.
- ❖ If you are going to seek God, then you have to be willing to withdraw yourself and seek the Father in prayer.
- ❖ Seeking God in all-night prayer allows for the one praying to receive clarity and direction about specific topics.
- ❖ Seeking God consistently and habitually will take you from being led by the Spirit of God to being empowered by the Spirit of God.

"**D**on't let past mistakes keep you from seeking God."

Billy Graham

CONCLUSION

What is the conclusion of *The Art of Seeking God*? Fear God and keep His commandments (Ecclesiastes 12:13). The one commandment you must strive to keep is found in 2 Chronicles 16:11. It reads, "Seek the Lord continually." When you embrace this commandment, you are then strengthened by God to carry out the other commandments in the Bible. Remember, seeking God is an art. A true artist spends many days, weeks, months, and years perfecting his/her craft. An artist has several options when creating an art piece. If his/her goal is to create a house, then they may use oil pastels, watercolor paint, digital painting, regular pencils, colored pencils, markers, and acrylic paint. The goal is to create a house using various art techniques.

Our goal is to seek God. When you and I use the many options (prayer, reading, meditating, etc.) available to us to seek God, then according to scripture we are going to find Him. Even when an artist messes up or becomes discouraged, they do not stop working on the art piece. They keep perfecting their piece of artwork. The same holds true for seeking God. You may mess up and sin, but you have to repent and get right back to seeking God. You may not encounter God on your timetable. That's okay! Keep seeking God because He has a timetable in place that has an exact time where He is going to reveal Himself to you. Keep perfecting your craft when it comes to seeking God.

Keep seeking! Seeking God is sacred time that should not be taken lightly or for granted. Seeking God is a precious time, so you must be attentive and focused. Hard work pays off. The goal of seeking is to develop a consistent relationship with Jesus Christ. Seeking God requires patience, diligence, discipline, and attentiveness. Seeking God is a skill that must be sharpened and perfected. Seeking God is a way of life. You must have a balance in the way you seek God. Seeking God will open the gates of heaven and allow God to pour into your life. Seeking God brings true deliverance. Every little step you take will bring you closer to God. Seek

God until heaven moves. Seek God until you know your destiny and purpose in life. Seek God and discover your gifts, skills, and talents. Seek God until you get the answer to that personal or group question. Seek God until He performs on your behalf. Let these words ring in your spirit, heart, and mind forever.

The final thought on seeking God is found in Jeremiah 29:11-13. The scripture reads,

> For I know the thoughts that I think toward you, saith the LORD, thoughts of peace, and not of evil, to give you an expected end. Then shall ye call upon me, and ye shall go and pray unto me, and I will hearken unto you. And ye shall seek me, and find me, when ye shall search for me with all your heart.

God has thoughts specifically designed about you. We know that thoughts become words and words become actions. I encourage you to seek God until He reveals the detailed thoughts that He has about you, to you. Understand, God sees the end from beginning. In other words, He sees your whole life. God is declaring in the scripture that if you call out to Him, He is going to answer you. God is saying that if you seek Him you are going to find Him. God has a plan for your life. The plan is amazing, and it will help you and those around you. Seek the Father while He may be found!

APPENDIX A

TWELVE DIFFERENT WAYS TO SEEK THE FATHER

(1) Seeking the Father via Reading the Word of God

Reading the Word of God is a top priority when it comes to seeking God. There are a lot of great ways to seek God, but if you are not reading the Bible and retaining biblical knowledge, then you are missing out on the essential thing that will allow you to grow as a Christian. Reading the Bible is mandatory for all believers. The Bible is our blueprint while living on earth. Someone once stated that BIBLE stands for Basic Instructions Before Leaving Earth. 1 Peter 2:2 states that as newborn babes we should desire the sincere milk of the word, that by it we may grow. Just like newborn babes need milk to grow, we too, as Christians, need to consume the Word of God as if it were milk. Reading the Bible is key for new converts. As new converts (and even seasoned saints), read the Bible so that you can understand God and how He relates to man. As you read, be a detective. Examine the Bible. Grasp the Bible. Understand the Bible. Take notes on what you read. Highlight your favorite stories, chapters, and verses.

As Christians, we should pray and seek God for the interpretation and revelation of scripture. Read the Word of God to know the context behind the stories. Read for enjoyment. (Beware of the peacock spirit [pride] that is on many of the saints of God.) Many Christians have not read the entire Bible, and some Christians have stopped reading the Bible. The Word of God is food and drink that allows believers to grow spiritually and naturally when eaten consistently. The Word of God is like water that will wash away every spot, wrinkle, and blemish. The Word of God will build you up and give you sustenance.

The Bible is a love story. Reading the Bible will help you to know and understand your Creator, Father God. From the book of Genesis to the book of Revelation you will see and understand the love that God has for His creation. The Bible contains an answer to every question that comes to mind. The Bible is a weapon when mixed with faith. The Bible is what you are to become. The Word was made flesh and dwelt among us full of grace and truth (John 1:14). The Bible is the written Word of God, but when you add the Spirit of God, the written Word comes to life. Then the Word brings change to your life and those around you. The Word of God can give you direction and advice on how to handle life's situations. The Word of God is filled with principles, commandments, laws, and truths that can give you godly knowledge, wisdom, and understanding.

APPLICATION: Read the Bible for fifteen minutes a day, thirty minutes a day, an hour a day. You know your schedule, start somewhere and began to read the Bible. Read the book of Proverbs and the book of John first. Then read the other gospels. Pray and ask God what you should read. Maybe the church you attend has a reading plan that consists of reading New and Old Testament scriptures each day. Regardless of the plan, I beseech you to read the Word of God.

(2)Seeking the Father via Studying the Word of God

Another way to seek God is by studying the Word of God. The word *study* means the cultivation of a particular branch of learning, to apply oneself to the acquisition of knowledge as by reading, investigation, and practice; to examine and investigate carefully. When you study, you labor; you put in work to receive an increased level of knowledge, wisdom, and understanding.

Studying the Word of God is deeper than reading because now you begin to absorb the Word, memorize the Word, understand the Word, investigate the Word, learn the Word, and reflect on the Word. When you study, you want to know something in a deeper sense. The Bible says in Proverbs 4:7, in all of your getting, get an understanding. In other words, when you study the Word of God you want to grasp, comprehend, and discern the Word of God. You want what you study to become meat and drink that sticks to your spiritual bones.

On top of getting an understanding, we must seek for revelation in the scriptures. 2 Timothy 2:15 says, "Study to show thyself approved unto God, a workman that needeth not to be ashamed, rightly dividing the word of truth." What does it mean to rightly divide the word of truth?

❖ Rightly dividing the Word means using the Bible in a way that gives clarity and meaning to the purposes of God.

❖ Rightly dividing the Word means using multiple scriptures that are suitable for any given topic.

❖ Rightly dividing the Word means using scriptures that brings clarity and understanding to life's situations.

❖ Rightly dividing the Word of God is taking the deeper things of God and making them plain using scriptures.

❖ Rightly dividing the Word of God means using the Word of God in a way that builds, perfects, sharpens and strengthens the Body of Christ.

❖ Rightly dividing the Word of God means using scriptures that brings life and not death to the hearer.

❖ Rightly dividing the Word of God requires the seeker to be in tune with the Holy Ghost.

❖ Rightly dividing the Word of God means applying the right scriptures to what is taking place in the earth.

Before you can rightly divide the Word of God, you have to study. The Holy Ghost is a Helper or a Guide. You have to put some work in first. You have to study. You have to labor in the Word of God. You have to get your tools (Bible, books, reference books, articles, websites, and videos). Studying takes time, dedication, patience, and focus. You have to be willing to set aside time to study. Then you have to be patient. Your goal to understand any given topic will come, but it takes time to get to that point.

I would compare studying to baking a pound cake or sweet potato pie from scratch. If it is your first time baking a pound cake or sweet potato pie, the end result might not taste like granny's or Uncle J's. The more you stay in the kitchen fine-tuning, that recipe will eventually lead to a product that you can share at the family barbecue. Studying is the same way. Starting off, you may get frustrated, overwhelmed, and ready to quit, but over the course of time, if you continue to study, you will comprehend, learn, and totally understand the topics that you are studying.

When I first started studying the Word of God, the things that I wrote on paper were totally elementary, confusing, and just off. But I kept pushing myself to study. One night, over the course of several weeks and a few months, the Holy Ghost came to visit. He breathed on what I was studying. What I began to write on paper made sense. The Holy Ghost was leading me and guiding me. This was a fantastic start for where I was at as a studier of the Word of God.

Then a few years went by and God put someone in my life who said, "You have to go deeper when you study." I then realized that there is surface studying and deep studying. You can study in the shallow end (a great starting point), but eventually you have to dive into the deeper waters (the end result for believers).

Remember, the Holy Ghost is the best Teacher. If you seek Him, He will give you the drive that will push you to study. The Holy Ghost uses people, so always be open when the man of God or woman of God gives you instruction and direction on how to study.

APPLICATION: Pick out a word, topic, person, or place in the Bible. Let's use the word *love*. Type or write all that you already know about love. Then find two or three Bible verses about love. Read those verses and then look up the Hebrew (Old Testament) or Greek (New Testament) definition of the word love. You will notice that the different words for love, depending on the scripture, will have a different meaning. Write those definitions down. Then study the context of the scripture. The context is dealing with the facts surrounding the given scripture you are studying. Write those facts down. Then how does the scripture apply to your life, your family's life, the church you attend, and your community. Write that information down. Then summarize the information that you gathered. Step away from your study for a few hours. Before you jump back into studying, pray and meditate on the topic of love. Allow the Holy Ghost to flood you with His thoughts on love. Allow the Holy Ghost to bring some other scriptures to the surface that line up with what you are studying. As you pray and meditate, you may receive an example of a life circumstance that feeds into what you are studying. Then, when you sit down for Round Two of studying, add the missing pieces that you gathered in your time of prayer and meditation. When you look back over your notes you will have accumulated a nice amount of information on love. You will be more well-versed on that topic. Now you just have to read it, study it, and commit it to memory. The above method is a basic formula for studying.

(3) Seeking the Father Via Prayer

Read 1 Corinthians 14; Jude 1:20; Acts 2:1-4

Praying is another way to seek God. Prayer is communication with God. You talk to Him and He talks to you. In 1 Corinthians 14:15, Paul said to pray with understanding. That means that you should pray in your native tongue or a learned language. You can say prayers of thanksgiving, repentance, petitions, and warfare. You can pray the scriptures. You can ask God for spiritual blessings and natural blessing. You can pray for people. You can pray for yourself. You can pray alone or in a group. You can pray aloud or to yourself. One man said that prayer is doing business with God.

1 Thessalonians 5:17 reads that we should pray without ceasing. The life of the believer should be that of prayer. How much prayer do you have in your prayer account? If you pray a lot, you will have much power. If you pray a little, you will have a little power. If you don't pray at all, then you will not have any power.

Prayer is your spiritual oil that keeps your engine running. Prayer is your spiritual juice that gives you strength. Prayer is your spiritual Gatorade that gives you energy. Regardless of how you pray, you have to "pray until you pray". Praying until you pray means pressing and pushing into prayer until you know and feel the Holy Ghost leading you as you pray.

The Bible makes it clear in James 5:16 that the effectual fervent prayer of a righteous man "availeth much." The verse is not only talking about the prayers of the righteous but the effectual fervent prayers of the righteous. There is a difference between praying and praying effectual fervent prayers.

Effectual fervent prayer is not about yelling and screaming, but it's about praying Spirit-led prayers with precision, passion, and power. Like our Savior, you must pray with authority. The effectual fervent prayer is a working prayer. It is a prayer where the one praying is literally operating in the spiritual realm. The prayer is intense, hot, and has a purpose. Effectual fervent prayers are Spirit-led prayers that shift atmospheres, heal nations, usher in repentance, and change situations. These types of prayers are so intense that some would say that the one praying is "on fire." The Bible says that ministers are flames of fire (Psalm 104:4; Hebrews 1:7), which means that the prayers that proceed from men and women of God should be fire. Fire is red hot and has the ability to permanently change or transform a person, situation, or region.

When you pray these prayers, pray with boldness and conviction. You have to believe and have faith when you pray. Some saints are intimidated by the way other saints pray. It does not have to be this way. Christian leaders must teach men, women, and the youth how to pray. Like any business, profession, or practice, the goal is growth. The goal is for saints to develop into ones who can pray like Elijah, Paul, Daniel, Jesus, and others. Remember, Elijah prayed seven times and then God sent the rain. Paul said we should pray with understanding and pray in tongues. He boasted that he did both more than others. Daniel prayed so much that an angel was sent to him personally to answer his prayer. Then you have Jesus who was always praying to the Father. No one person just started praying in a mature manner. The disciples wanted to learn how to pray. They had no shame and no pride.

You and me, like the disciples, must develop our prayer lives. Just like Jesus taught them, hopefully, there are men and women of God around you who can teach you how to pray. As you listen and learn, allow praying to become a habitual part of your lifestyle. The goal is to pray in private and public with great confidence. Understand that prayer is talking to God, but as you mature in Christ your prayers should also mature. Don't be intimidated, but press in to God and develop your prayer life.

Praying in the Holy Ghost, or speaking in tongues, is also communication with God. Praying in the Holy Ghost or speaking in tongues is very fruitful. When you pray in the Holy Ghost, you build yourself up. When you pray in the Holy Ghost, you pray the mysteries of God into manifestation. When you pray in the Holy Ghost, the devil and his evil host cannot understand what is being spoken. When you pray in the Holy Ghost, you pray the will of God, because you are not praying but your spirit is praying. Paul was big on speaking in tongues. He said that we should pray with understanding and pray without understanding. He boasted that he prayed in tongues more than other people. Understand that when you pray in tongues, you are praying the direct will of God. Push yourself to pray in your heavenly language consistently and often.

The final thought on prayer is like Jesus said, "Not my will but yours (the Father's) will be done." (Luke 22:42) When you pray and God answers, you have to obey. What you hear in prayer, you practice in your daily life. Remember, prayer is two-way communication. When you pray, God hears you; you should hear Him and obey.

APPLICATION: Develop a prayer schedule where you are able to pray to the Father. Pray in the morning, afternoon, and/or evening. Pray for fifteen minutes, thirty minutes, sixty minutes, or longer. The main thing is that you have to start praying. Get out a piece of paper and write down ten to fifteen prayer targets. Some prayer targets can include yourself, your spouse, church, family, friends, enemies, career, life goals, wisdom, wealth, and more. Once you have written your prayer targets on paper, try to identify some scriptures that line up with each prayer target. Then, turn on some worship music. Keep the volume low. Burn some candles and some incense. Then, start off by praying on each target for thirty to sixty seconds. After your pray for the first prayer target, start praying for

THE ART OF SEEKING GOD

the next prayer target. After a few days, you will notice a change in how you pray and you will notice that you are spending more than one minute praying for each prayer target. Understand, you don't have to have candles, incenses, and/or music to pray. Those things enhance the atmosphere. The point is you have to pray and pray often.

Paul stated in 1 Corinthians 14:15 that we should pray in the spirit or in tongues. He went on to state in verse 18 that he spoke in tongues more than others. From these two verses, I encourage you to set aside time to pray in the Holy Ghost. You can start off praying for five minutes in the Holy Ghost and then work your way up to larger time frames. The work you put into to seeking God in your heavenly language will determine how much God reveals Himself to you. If you have not been filled with the Holy Ghost with the evidence of speaking in tongues, then head to the nearest altar near you. Men and women of God are waiting to pray with you so that you can receive the gift of the Holy Ghost.

(4)Seeking the Father via Fasting

In all that we do as Christians, we must be led by the Spirit of God (Romans 8:14). The one event in history that always grabs my attention is when the loyal disciples of Jesus were not able to cast out a demon. Besides their unbelief, Jesus made it plain to His disciples that some deliverances can only happen by prayer and fasting.

The question is, "What is fasting?" Fasting is a voluntary abstinence from food and/or drink; a time to put away all types of earthly pleasures; a time to focus your spirit, soul, and body on God. Fasting is a sacrifice that will bring you closer to God quickly when done the correct way. Fasting kills the flesh, or the appetites of the flesh. Fasting makes your spirit man more sensitive to the Spirit of God. Fasting can allow the Spirit of God to be the head of your life and your flesh the tail.

As a believer, you must dominate and destroy your flesh and make it line up with the commandment to seek the Lord continuously. Jesus fasted. Moses fasted. King David fasted. Paul fasted.

Several others in the Word of God fasted. Fasting was common in the Bible days and it must become common again, today, in the kingdom of God. When you fast, make it a point to pray, read your Bible, listen to worship music, meditate, perform good deeds, soak in God's presence, etc.

There are many natural and spiritual benefits to fasting. Fasting gives you a 'God conscience.' Fasting kills one's earthly and sensual appetites and increases one's spiritual appetite for God. Fasting gives you spiritual power to operate in the power of God. In the Bible, when men and women of God fasted, there was a specific reason for the fast. Esther fasted in the hope that God would deliver her and the children of Israel. David fasted in the hope that God would heal his son. Moses fasted when he received the commandments from God.

There should be a reason as to why you are fasting. The Bible is full of information about fasting. All in all, fasting will kill your flesh and allow your spirit man to get closer to God. Fasting will empower you to be victorious over people, devilish spirits, and things in your life. Fasting will give you divine solutions to demonic problems that may be in your life or around you. Fasting and praying will still you, calm you, and allow you to hear and receive clearly from the Father. Isaiah 58 is filled with details about fasting. *See Appendix B for more details on fasting.*

APPLICATION: Fasting is a very serious matter. You need to connect with your local church. They should have something in place regarding how they approach fasting. At my church, we have all new citizens take a set of classes called Prayer and Fasting. These classes last six to eight weeks and they teach and train new citizens on how to pray and fast. At the conclusion of those classes, citizens are allowed to fast. The recommendation for new converts is to fast from 6am – 6pm, drinking only water. That can take place once a week. Then, new converts can try fasting two to three times a week from 6am – 6pm. My church has a corporate fast from time to time. A corporate fast can last one day, three days, ten days, or longer. More seasoned saints should try fasting for twenty-four hours without food and/or water. Once again, I strongly recommend that you join a local church and fall under the tutelage of how that church conducts fasting.

(5)Seeking the Father Via Meditation

Meditation is another way to seek God. Practicing meditation from a Christian point of view is what allowed me to hear the Spirit of God, discern atmospheres, and be more sensitive to the spiritual activity taking place around me. Meditation is a mental exercise, an act of worship, healthy for the body, and spiritual. In Joshua 1:8 it reads, "This book of the law shall not depart out of thy mouth; but thou shalt meditate therein day and night, that thou mayest observe to do according to all that is written therein, for then thou shalt make thy way prosperous, and then thou shalt have good success." Meditation is a time of deep thought, concentration, or reflection on the Word of God. 1 Timothy 4:13-15 reads, "Till I come, give attendance to reading, to exhortation, to doctrine. Neglect not the gift that is in thee, which was given thee by prophecy, with the laying on of the hands of the presbytery. Meditate upon these things; give thyself wholly to them; that thy profiting may appear to all."

Meditation is when you reflect, think, or ponder on the things of God. Meditation is when you let the things of God revolve around in your mind. Meditation is when you use your imagination for the things of God. You can meditate on the scripture, prophecies, sermons, teachings, the awesomeness of God, who you are in God, and several other things associated with the kingdom of God. Meditation is a time to monitor your thoughts. Meditation disciplines your mind.

In Genesis 24:63, Isaac went out in a field to meditate, and when he looked up his wife was before him. Meditation will allow you to hear what the Spirit of God is saying more clearly. Christian meditation is not the same as Hindu and Buddhism meditation. Christian meditation is not talked about a lot, but it is rooted and grounded in the Word of God. Meditation is a spiritual practice and should not be taken lightly. This spiritual practice can yield several benefits to your spiritual body and physical body when practiced the correct way.

APPLICATION: Before you meditate, pray over yourself. That way, you are protected and covered by the blood of Jesus. Anoint your head with oil. Burn some incense, preferably frank-incense (optional). It is always best to pray over your incense too, seeing how it's not always made by Christians. Sit cross-legged on the floor or on your couch. If you need to just sit normal, that will also work. Play soft meditation music in the background (worship, soaking, and instrumentals—optional) Be comfortable. Take one deep breath in and release all of your thoughts. Inhale and exhale three times. Think about calmness and peace. Inhale and exhale three times. Think about Jesus Christ. Think about inhaling all of God. Inhale and exhale three times. For fifteen minutes, meditate on specific Bible verses, prophesies spoken over your life, responsibilities as a Christian, your gifts, your skills, your talents, or your ministry. As you meditate, listen for God's voice. In all, a fifteen-minute meditation is a great start. After a few weeks of mastering fifteen minutes, then increase your meditation time to thirty, forty-five, and sixty minutes. Once again, I strongly recommend that you connect with a seasoned Christian that has experience meditating.

(6)Seeking the Father via Praise

2 Chronicles 20:20-22 reads,

> And they rose early in the morning, and went forth into the wilderness of Tekoa: and as they went forth, Jehoshaphat stood and said, Hear me, O Judah, and ye inhabitants of Jerusalem; Believe in the LORD your God, so shall ye be established; believe his prophets, so shall ye prosper. And when he had consulted with the people, he appointed singers unto the Lord, and that should praise the beauty of holiness, as they went out before the army, and to say, Praise the Lord; for his mercy endureth

forever. And when they began to sing and to praise, the Lord set ambushments against the children of Ammon, Moab, and Seir, which were come against Judah; and they were smitten.

Praise is a giving thanks to God, and at the same time it is warring against the enemy. One Hebrew word for praise, *yadah* (3034), means hold out the hand, to throw a stone or an arrow at or away; to revere with extended hands, confess, give thanks.

Praise is a form of warfare. Just like in biblical movies and movies such as *Braveheart*, or better yet, *Gladiator*, arrows were shot forth into the enemy's camp before hand-to-hand combat took place. The arrows destroyed a host of soldiers. When we praise God, we give glory to God and we shoot arrows into the enemy's camp. Praise is an aerial attack in the spiritual realm before hand-to-hand combat takes place, which is when the Word of God goes forth in power and demonstration of the Holy Ghost. Praising God brings honor to God and it is an offensive assault on the enemy. When you say or shout "Jesus" or "Hallelujah," you shoot arrows into the enemy's camp. When you say shout out a praise, you send fiery arrows into the enemy's camp. When you praise God in the good times, and especially the bad times, you send a barrage of fiery arrows into the enemy's camp.

Praising God is two-fold. On the one hand, we are giving honor, thanks, and glory to God with our mouths and hands; but on the other hand we're striking death blows to the enemy when we praise God. When giants manifest in your life, the focus must be on praising God. You cannot allow giants to intimidate, control, manipulate, or strike fear into you. You must praise God, and as you praise God, the giants in your life will coming crashing down.

Let's look at the life of King David while on the battlefield with the giant, Goliath. Goliath and the demonic host backing him began to mock the Living God and his warriors. David, at the time just a young shepherd boy, grabbed five smooth stones from the brook. He hurled one smooth stone at the enemy. That one smooth stone destroyed the giant that was facing God's people. Here we see a natural manifestation of praise (yadah) taking place.

David slung, hurled, or threw the stone at the Philistine and he came crashing down. Even in current times, when we praise God, the giants around us will come crashing down.

The word praise has many meanings. You can praise God with your mouth, clapping, singing, jumping, running, kneeling, lifting your hands, and playing instruments. David said in Psalm 9, "I will praise thee, O Lord, with my whole heart; I will show forth all thy marvelous works." David was serious about praising the Lord because He did so many amazing things in David's life.

Just like David, many of us have faced death, prison time, giants, sickness, rejection, enemies, mountainous situations, etc. Like David, we all have dealt with sin in our lives. To see God deliver us and save us time and time again is the reason why we praise God or should praise God so hard. He is worthy, amazing, and altogether lovely.

APPLICATION: Praise is a serious time, but also a joyous time. You can praise God with or without music. Set aside some time each day. Play some Christian music that praises God. While the music is playing, begin to praise God with your mouth. You can sing along with the music and/or you can say things like:

1. I bless your name, Jesus!
2. Hallelujah!
3. You are worthy, Jesus!
4. Glory, glory, glory!

When you begin to praise Jesus over and over again, it becomes real. You might start crying and/or feeling really happy. It's okay. Keep praising Him because he is worthy of our praise.

(7)Seeking the Father via Worship

1 Chronicles 16:29 reads, "Give unto the Lord the glory due unto his name: bring an offering, and come before him: worship the Lord in the beauty of holiness." Worship is a high form of reverence and honor given to God. In Matthew 4:10, Jesus told

Satan, "Thou shalt worship the Lord thy God, and him only shalt thou serve."

Worshipping God is when you surrender your will to God's will. Worshipping God is normally associated with being in church and takes place at key times during the service. During that time, you will find believers worshipping God from a number of different positions (standing with hands raised towards heaven, kneeling, lying prostrate on the floor, or bowing down with their face to the ground). Understand, that you can worship God at church, home, on you job and/or where ever you are led to worship God.

Worshipping is also a time when one will shut up, focus, and listen. Worship can lead to the presence of God manifesting. There is always purpose behind God's presence.

We read in Exodus 33:14-15 that when Moses went into the presence of God he came away with a purpose or objective for himself or the children of Israel. Worshipping God unlocks the presence of God and God's presence is always followed by the purpose of God for one's life. Worship is not only a time to focus on God, but it is a lifestyle that happens 24/7.

John 4:23-24 reads, "But the hour cometh, and now is, when the true worshippers shall worship the Father in spirit and in truth: for the Father seeketh such to worship him. God is a spirit and they that worship him must worship him in spirit and in truth."

Worshipping God in spirit and truth means that the believer is living a lifestyle that is rooted and grounded in things of the Spirit of God and things that deal with truth. That means that the believer's spirit is being led by the Spirit of God in words and actions. That means that the believer is able to receive truth on a God level. A God level means you are able to know and understand what is true regardless of the situation. Worshipping God in spirit and in truth means you are able to apply spiritual principles to your life and live a mature life that is free from the falsehood and deception of this world.

APPLICATION: Worship God at your house. Burn some candles, burn some incense, and play some Christian music if you have some. If you do not have the above, that is okay. Those items help with the atmosphere, but are not always needed or accessible.

Regardless, begin to thank God and praise Him for what He is doing in your life. This may take some time, and that is okay. You want an encounter, a visitation, not a microwave moment. Praise God intentionally! Your praise will eventually turn into worship. You are going to feel the Spirit of God come into the room. It's at this moment or place where the music may be playing, or it may not be playing. The candles may have burnt out and the smoke from the incense is no longer hitting the air. You will find yourself still. You can lay prostrate on the floor. You can stand with your hands extended to heaven. You can bow down. You may be on your knees. Regardless of your position, you are in a surrendered state. This is the time to focus on God and bask in His presence. Let Him minister to you as you yield to Him. Be open to receive from the Spirit of God. This is a worship experience. When you finish the worship experience, you may be energized or you may feel tired. Regardless of how you feel, you have to get back to living a life where you are relevant to humanity.

(8) Seeking the Father via Music

Another way of seeking God involves listening to music. When the right music is played, it can create an atmosphere for meditation, praise, and worship. When the right type of music is played God can minister to you and God's people.

I remember when I got saved back in February of 1996. I would be at home by myself from time to time, and I literally would put on some praise and worship music. I would dance like King David did when he praised the living God in a pair of "old school" boxers before the people. The music that I played at the time literally shifted the atmosphere for the presence of God to manifest in my house. The music was anointed and pure. The music lifted up the name of Jesus. I felt the Holy Ghost. At times, I would find myself full of joy and excitement. At other times, I would find myself in awe and in reverence (fear) of the Lord. At times, I would just lay on the floor in a still position with tears soaking up the carpet. Some Christian music is so anointed that, while listening to it, conviction, humility, and forgiveness will flood your soul. You will find yourself longing to stay right there in the presence of God. You will find yourself convicted about wanting to live holy, godly, and righteous. Listening to Christian music opens up the door for you to commune with God. You speak to Him and He speaks to you. Some Christian music is so anointed that I cannot even put into words how it makes me feel.

2 Kings 3:15 reads,

> "But now bring me a minstrel. And it came to pass, when the minstrel played, that the hand of the Lord came upon him."

In the above verse, the prophet of God asked for a minstrel to be brought to him. When the minstrel played, the hand of God came upon the prophet. The minstrel was one that played a string instrument. When the instrument was played, all of God entered the atmosphere and the supernatural took place. From there, the prophet began to declare the word of the Lord.

In 1 Samuel 16, an evil spirit came upon King Saul. The evil spirit only departed when David played the harp. The anointed music that David played brought deliverance to King Saul.

Godly music played by men and women of God has the power to usher in the presence of God and bring deliverance to those in attendance. The right Christian music played in public or private can shift the atmosphere and bring deliverance to the listener.

Ephesians 5:19 reads,

> "Speaking to yourselves in psalms and hymns and spiritual songs, singing and making melody in your heart to the Lord:"

As Christians, we will either have a song to sing or the Holy Spirit will drop a new song in our spirit to sing. In I Kings 4:32 it reads that Solomon wrote 1,005 songs. Wow! Song writers, just think about the songs that God wants to birth out of your spiritual womb. Sometimes the right Christian music can express the way you feel in your inner man. Sometimes God will talk to you through music. Playing Christian music can bring the presence of God to you for comfort, conviction, edification, deliverance, and peace. We should sing Christian music unto the Lord. Every time we sing, there should not always be an attached agenda. We should get in the habit of just singing unto the Lord because He is a magnificent King.

Colossians 3:16 reads,

> "Let the word of Christ dwell in you richly in all wisdom; teaching and admonishing one another in psalms and hymns and spiritual songs, singing with grace in your hearts to the Lord."

Note: There are all kinds of genres (techno, rap, country, jazz, contemporary, gospel, electro, spiritual, etc.) when it comes to music that glorifies God. Each genre of music is performed by people from all nations. The music is performed in different languages by different ethnic groups. The music may sound foreign or hideous to one group, but to another group and God the music is glorious, pure, and acceptable. God has people from many different folds who create music that touches the heart of God and His people. All musicians are in search of that one sound that caters to all people. If that sound is discovered or not discovered, let's be mindful that there are different genres that are able to usher in the presence of God and turn the hearts of man back to God.

APPLICATION: As of March 2020, you have access to all kinds of music via streaming services like YouTube, Spotify, SiriusXM, Apple Music, and many more. Music can still be downloaded and CDs can be purchased. Depending on who you know, you may be able to access albums and cassette tapes. Find your music source and find some good Christian music that includes praise, worship, rap, gospel, contemporary, etc. Whatever your favorite music genre may be, find it and start listening to Christian music. The music can be live at church, at a concert, or some random place. You can listen to music wherever you are, but I would suggest that you set aside some time when you are able to enjoy Christian music in the confines of your own home. Let the music minister to you. Sometimes the music will make you smile. At other times you may find yourself crying uncontrollably and you won't even know why. You will notice that some of your best moments as a Christian will be enjoying some amazing Christian music.

(9) Seeking the Father via Church Attendance

Reference verses: 1 Corinthians 12:28, 14:4-35; Ephesians 3:10; Matthew 16:18; Acts 5:1

Hebrews 10:25 makes it clear that we should not forsake the assembly of the believers. We understand that the true church is built with the hearts of man and not the hands of man. We, as believers, *are* the church. We may gather in a building or under a bridge. It is a blessing that we are still able to go to a local building that has been labeled as a church. We can gather at a house, a school, or a church building. We cannot forget about each other as believers. We must come together and be the church.

David said, "I was glad when they said unto me, let us go into the house of the Lord." Jesus went to the synagogue faithfully. Paul preached in churches faithfully and set up churches all over the Gentile region. The Bible says that where any two or three of you gather that Jesus will be in the midst. The Bible goes on to say that we are the temple of the living God and that He would dwell and walk amongst us. God lives inside each believer.

When we come together as the church, we make up the body of Christ. Each believer is a citizen of the kingdom and a member of the body of Christ. At church, the focus is on seeing souls become disciples. As disciples, our focus should be on serving. As we serve in the local church, we should be taught the ways of the kingdom. The Bible says in Matthew 16:18 that, "upon this rock" (this sure foundation, which is Jesus Christ), "I will build my church and the gates of hell shall not prevail against it." When the church, the body of believers, comes together, we grow stronger, tighter, bolder, more powerful, and when that happens, all things are possible. The church is where one is converted, edified, perfected, exhorted, taught, instructed, trained, equipped, warned, and rebuked if necessary, but it should all be done in love. Finally, the church is the place where you go to meet God. The church is a place of corporate seeking. When we come together to seek God corporately, we can experience God on a greater level.

APPLICATION: Find a church home and attend it faithfully. Not only that, but get involved and let your presence be felt. Churches are always being perfected or matured. Just know that God is working on all of us. Be the difference-maker at your church. Be the light! Be the salt! Be the one who is faithful, loving, holy, and full of the Holy Ghost. If you are a new convert and you need help finding a church, please reach out to me via email and I will help you find a church in your hometown.

(10) Seeking the Father via Reading Materials

Reference verses: 1 Timothy 4:13; 2 Timothy 4:13

In the above two verses, Paul makes it clear that we as believers should read. He stressed to his brethren to bring him his books. If we fast-forward to this present day, we have several types of reading materials. If Paul were alive today, he would be consumed with reading books, journals, media, blogs, articles, magazines, etc. When you read, you learn about God's creation, the good and the bad. Reading or being well-versed on a number of different topics makes us more knowledgeable. When one is more knowledgeable, he or she is able to converse with people from all walks of life. We are called to be all things to all people.

When you read, you are seeking the Father because the Holy Ghost is inside of you. He is teaching you as you read and allowing things to make sense to you. As you read, He is helping you to connect the dots. Do you remember the movie *Superman* or *The Matrix*? In those movies, baby Superman and Neo went through a training period where they were downloaded with all kinds of information. Over the course of those movies, the two were able to connect the dots and make sense of the world that they were living in at the time. As believers, we are the same way. We have to consume reading materials and allow the Holy Ghost to help us to connect the dots. As we connect the dots, we will learn more about God and His creation.

APPLICATION: I hope you have access to a five-fold ministry gift, an elder, a bishop, or some man or woman of God who can assist you in choosing spiritually appropriate books. If you do not have anyone, then I would suggest reading *Spiritual Leadership: Principles of Excellence* by J. Oswald Sanders. Reading the Bible along with this book will get you started on the right track to getting "discipled" the correct way.

(11) Seeking God via Different Media Types

Seeing, watching, and listening to the preached and taught Word of God via websites, compact discs (CDs), digital video discs (DVDs), MP3 players, streaming, applications (apps), and social media is another way of seeking God. Repetition is one of the best ways to learn. Listening to or watching sermons over and over gets the "rhema" word spoken into your heart and spirit. We retain 10% of what we hear. We retain 30% to 40% of what we see *and* hear. It is a blessing to be able to listen to and watch sermons over and over again. As you listen to and watch these sermons, you should remain prayerful about them. As you listen, you should take notes. The notes can become prayer targets, principles to live by, and revelation that grows you. God can and will give a deeper revelation to some of the sermons and teachings. What you give attendance to will be what God gives you understanding about. We serve a deep God! Whatever is spoken can always be taken deeper. The Bible says, "He that hath an ear, let him hear." (Matthew 11:15) There are numerous preaching and teaching topics available to us. As you seek the Father, focus on seeking God via different media types that will lead to your growth in the natural and the spiritual.

APPLICATION: There are a lot of good preachers and teachers on social media and YouTube. I would recommend Bishop T.D. Jakes, Apostle Tudor Bismark, Prophet Cornelius Hale, Dr. Cindy Trimm, and the late Dr. Myles Monroe, as men and women of God who can provide kingdom doctrine that will further your growth as a Christian. Choose one of the above and listen to their preached messages or teaching. As you listen, take notes and apply the content to your daily life.

(12) Seeking God via Keeping Your Mind on God

Romans 8:5, 12:2; Matthew 22:37; 1 Corinthians 2:16; 2 Timothy 1:7; I Peter 3:8; Isaiah 26:3

As Christians, we must understand that our mind is very powerful. I liken the mind to the White House. The White House is a key place in this world, where decisions are made that can make or break a person, city, state, country, continent, and the world for that matter. Each individual mind holds the same type of power as the White House. It's in our mind where we make decisions that either make or break us as individuals. What we do as individuals affects the people around us directly and indirectly. The decisions that we make in our mind will push us closer to God or the devil. The goal of all Christians is to have the mind of Christ. As Christians, we must seek God by training our mind to stay focused on Him. As Christians, we want the mind of Christ. The Bible says that God will keep him in perfect peace whose mind is stayed on Him because you trust in Him (Isaiah 26:3). We should all be striving for the mind of Christ. As a result of that, we should monitor our thoughts. We should arrest devilish ideas and fill our mind with godly ideas. As a man thinketh, so is he (Proverbs 23:7). You think as a man and you will perform like a man. You think like God and you will perform like God. You must have a strong godly conscience that will bring ungodly thoughts into obedience with God's word. As you seek God via the above methods, your mind will begin to take on the mind of Christ. You want your seek to be so strong that no matter what you are doing, your mind is focused on God.

APPLICATION: The mind of Christ is a spiritual mind that receives spiritual intelligence that is relevant to the spiritual world and natural world. If you want to have the mind of Christ, do the following things:

1. Read and study what the Bible says about the mind of Christ.
2. Fellowship with (or hang around) men and women of God who can help your growth in the faith.
3. Read your Bible more than you do other things. By doing this, all of your stray thoughts will be about the Word of God.
4. Pray and meditate daily. Make it a habitual practice.
5. Listen to worship music, and while listening, just soak in the presence of God. Some would call it soaking music because the goal is to fully immerse your entire being into the worship experience. Close your eyes and totally focus your entire being on God.
6. Read books about getting or receiving the mind of Christ.
7. Avoid putting yourself in environments and being around people who are negative, anti-Christ, and/or unrighteous.

APPENDIX B

BENEFITS OF FASTING FOR THE NATURAL BODY

When you fast, you are giving many organs in the body a rest. These organs include the stomach, intestines, pancreas, gallbladder, and liver. This allows the most important organ, the liver, to spend more time cleaning up the toxins that are released into the blood and creating many new substances for our body to use. With less energy going to the process of digesting and processing food, the body will focus on cleaning out toxins.

"Side effects" of detoxification include: headache, fatigue, irritability at times, dizziness, and lightheadedness. Since senses are enhanced, some common sounds like TV, music, ticking clocks, and a running refrigerator may become irritating. The sense of smell is also exaggerated. The tongue of some people will develop a thick white, yellow, or grayish coating, which can be scraped or brushed off. Bad breath and displeasing tastes in the mouth, foul-smelling urine or stools, skin odor and eruptions, digestive upset, flatulence (gas), nausea, vomiting, insomnia, bad dreams, negative thoughts, doubts as to whether fasting is really the right thing to be doing, are all possible but will not necessarily happen. The degree to which your body eliminates toxins will depend upon how you have taken care of your body nutritionally in the past. You can help your fast by not fighting against what the body is doing and resting when your body tells you to rest. This is one reason why fasting is an inconvenience to many of us—we have forgotten how to rest and let our body restore itself. We are a busy and active culture that does not take the time to rest and restore, both physically and spiritually.[1]

NOTES

Introduction

1. "Trends and Statistics", https://www.drugabuse.gov/related-topics/trends-statistics#supplemental-references-for-economic-costs (accessed February 10, 2020).

Chapter 1

1. GodRules.net, s.v. "zeal", http://www.godrules.net/library/kjvstrongs/kjvstrongsisa37.html (accessed April 4, 2019).

Chapter 2

1. Dictionary.com, s.v. "art", https://www.dictionary.com/browse/art?s=t (accessed April 4, 2019).

Chapter 4

1. "Thirst, Sheep and Shepherds", http://www.raisingsheep.net/what-do-sheep-eat.html (accessed December 2, 2019).

2. Linda Gill, "What Do Sheep Eat? Sheep Food and Pasture – Raising Sheep", https://beingwoven.org/2016/03/11/thirst-sheep-and-shepherds/ (accessed December 1, 2019).

Appendix B

1. Claudia Meydrech, "The Happy Nutritionist", http://www.happynutritionist.com/2013/01/fasting.html (accessed October 4, 2018).

ABOUT THE AUTHOR

Aaron M. M. Butler M. Ed. is an ordained Elder at The City of David Church under the covering of Prophet Cornelius Hale, located in Columbus, Ohio. He received salvation at age of 20 on February 11,1996. As a practicing Christian, he believes in the Word of God. He believes in God the Father, Jesus the Son, and the Holy Spirit. He believes in the execution of the Five-Fold Ministry. He believes the love of Jesus has the power to transform lives. He believes in salvation; be saved from your sins and saved to your purpose in God. He believes that you do not have to walk in condemnation, but that you can learn to see God the way that He sees you. He has over ten years of experience as a church leader. He believes in the servant leadership model when it comes to serving God's people. He received his master's degree in Educational Administration from Ashland University and his bachelor's degree in Elementary Education from Wittenberg University. Aaron has over 20 years of experience as a teacher and building principal. He loves reaching and teaching inner city youth. In his spare time, he enjoys spending time with his family/friends, watching movies, sports, reading, and serving people in the community. Aaron currently resides in Pickerington, Ohio with his wife and two sons.

CPSIA information can be obtained
at www.ICGtesting.com
Printed in the USA
BVHW050752240423
662923BV00014B/789